D0884095

SUZANNE VALADON

Suzanne Valadon

BY JEANINE WARNOD

COLLECTOR'S EDITION
Bound in Genuine Leather

The Easton Press
NORWALK, CONNECTICUT

Translated from the French by:

SHIRLEY JENNINGS

Collection Published under the direction of:

MADELEINE LEDIVELEC-GLOECKNER

Photographs: Atelier 53, Paris - Atelier 80, Paris - Bulloz, Paris - Société Detaille, Monte-Carol - Stan Franzos, Pittsburgh - André Godin, Troyes - Jacqueline Hyde, Paris - Georges Kriloff, Lyons - Otto E. Nelson, New York - Nicolas Petit, Paris - Service Photographique du Musée National d'Art Moderne, CNAC Georges Pompidou, Paris - Service Photographique de la Réunion des Musées Nationaux, Paris - G. Soirat, Menton - Studio R. Scwartz, Benançon

Title page: SELF-PORTRAIT, 1916
Oil on canvas, 18 1/8" x 14" (46 x 38 cm)
Private collection

THE FUTURE UNVEILED, 1912. Oil on canvas, 24 3/4″ × 51 1/8″ (63 × 130 cm)
Musée Petit Palais, Geneva

Suzanne Valadon was a frequent visitor to our home at 60 rue Caulaincourt. My father, André Warnod, often invited his painter friends for a meal and Suzanne would come to lunch, accompanied by her husband, André Utter. At the time she was living only a stone's throw away at 11 avenue Junot in a villa bought for her son, Maurice Utrillo, by the Bernheims, the art dealers, who were already selling his pictures for large sums.

I was only a child then, and Suzanne seemed to me to be tiny and very old, with her wrinkled face and gray hair cut in a fringe. Dressed in a large cloak draped firmly around her shoulders and a felt hat thrust down over her forehead, she made a distinctly eccentric impression, mannish and gypsy-like. I was intimidated by the piercing eyes behind the glasses that seemed to look straight through you, and her habit of saying exactly what she thought in a few well-chosen words. She would tell the most extraordinary stories, at one moment bursting out laughing and the next inveighing against the injustice of people in high places, the «dirty tricks» played by painters, and the «fiddles» perpetrated by dealers. Impulsive, always ready

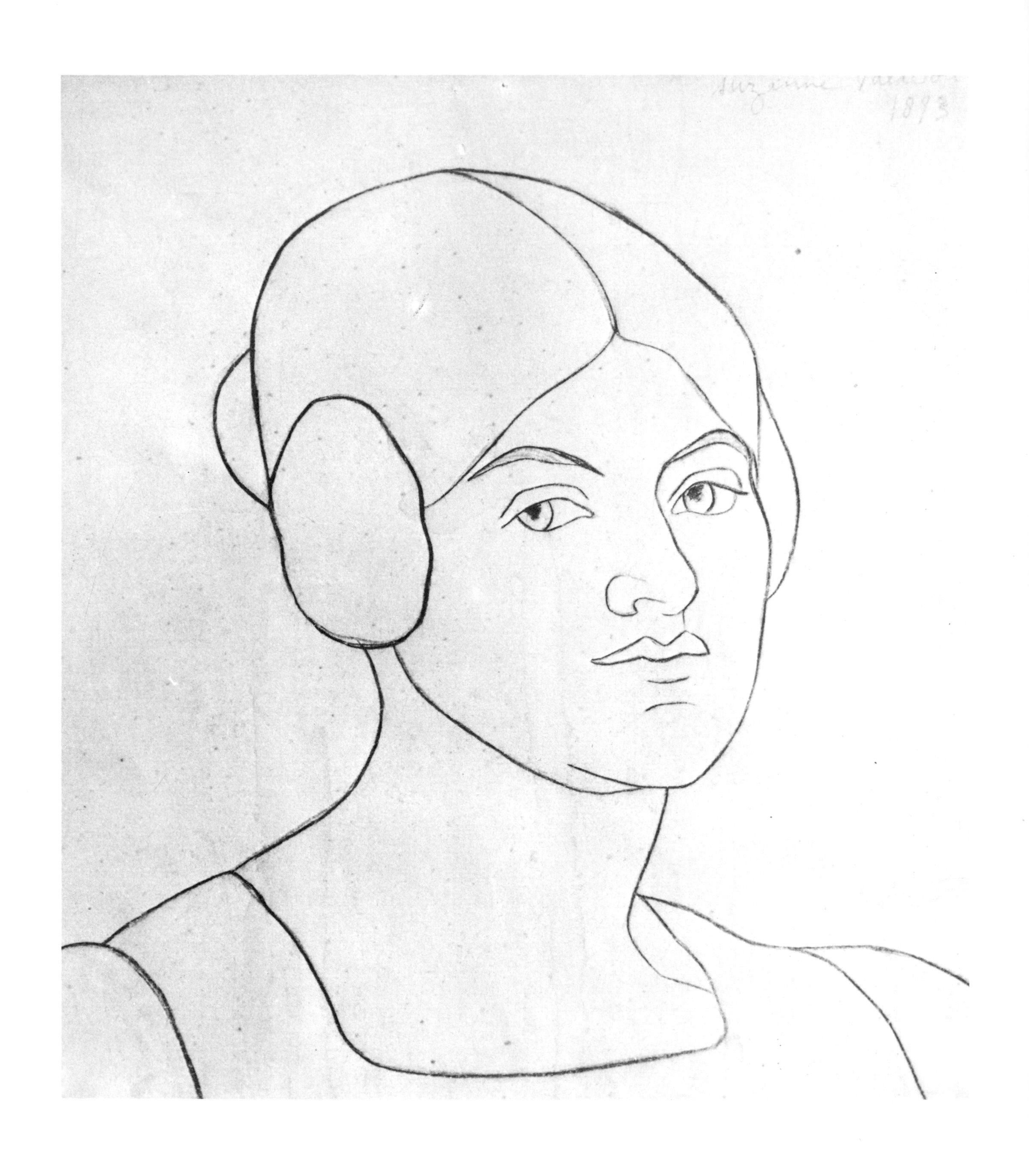

Self-Portrait, 1893. Black crayon, 9 7/8" × 9" (25 × 23 cm). Private collection (Photo Hachette)

SELF-PORTRAIT, 1902. Red chalk, 7 3/4″ × 5 1/8″ (20 × 13 cm). Collection Dina Vierny, Paris

to explode with anger, she was as extravagant in her generosity toward her friends as she was vehement in her exasperation at the unfairness of life.

One day she wanted to paint my portrait, but a few months before I had behaved so badly with Pascin that my parents regretfully refused, out of pity for both painter and model.

In the thirties I would see Suzanne taking her dogs for a walk in the «maquis,» as the still-unbuilt-up areas of the avenue Junot had been referred to when she was young. Already the little wooden shacks had given way to private houses. Poulbot had built his studio there, and Daragnès had set up his printing works, while Camoin and Gen Paul lived at the top of the avenue, at the corner of the rue Girardon. The artists and poets were fond of this attractive area, with its air of middle class prosperity unusual on the Butte. Suzanne Valadon enjoyed a period of affluent Bohemianism at the villa, after many years of poverty. She had come to Paris from her native province, Limousin, at the age of five, and almost all her work was done within the confines of Montmartre.

She had countless different addresses from the boulevard Rochechouart to the rue du Poteau, from the rue Tourlaque to the rue du Mont-Cenis, and from the impasse Guelma to the rue Cortot and the avenue Junot. The places where she spent her time were not far apart: the Lapin Agile, place Pigalle, the Moulin Rouge, the Moulin de la Galette, Adèle's restaurant and all the studios of the painters for whom she posed – but together they make up a long road traveled in the course of seventy years, full of obstacles and optimism, struggles and loneliness.

FATHER UNKNOWN

The first self-portrait* of Suzanne Valadon in 1883 shows her at the age of eighteen, with a serious, uncompromising face, strong features, and a proud, self-confident gaze above a sensual mouth. She looks as if she is prepared to face all difficulties and is utterly certain of her own mind.

But what is it that she wants out of life? To express herself freely, and satisfy to the full her many different passions? In her black dress, with her hair pulled back behind her ears, without artifice or affectation, she appears as upright and fiercely independent as she would remain until her death in 1938. I have seen her last identity card, which reads as follows: 1 meter 54 centimeters tall; eyes blue; nose turned-up, crooked, short; complexion mat.

Her life was like a serial film – a mixture of poverty and melodrama, with an accompaniment of circus music, against the background of Montmartre. Suzanne's strong character as woman, mother and artist developed in unusual circumstances. According to the friends in whom she confided, the episodes in her youth would have filled several books, for Suzanne was a mythomaniac and enjoyed inventing her life history, so that her stories were never the same from one day to the next.

When anyone asked her about her past, she would unearth the relevant letters but, instead of reading them, would burn them – to her visitor's surprise and dismay. Did she want to conceal the truth, obscure herself in mystery or discourage people who asked too many questions? She claimed that her head was shaped like a sugarloaf because her birth had been as difficult as her early life. And surely such a statement implies a total rejection of complacency. All the stories she told reveal a boundless imagination. The anecdotes are interesting for the light they shed on her character, but they are not much help in establishing the true facts of the case.

The following is an extract from the register of births in the Bessines-sur-Gartempe town hall:

«The year eighteen-hundred and sixty-five, on the twenty-third of September, at four o'clock in the evening, We, Pierre Paul, Emile DUMONTEIL, Mayor, acting as Registrar in the commune of BESSINES, chief town of the canton, arrondissement of Bellac, in the department of Haute-Vienne, received the visit of François Poignand, blacksmith, aged thirty-eight, residing

---

* See p. 10

Maurice Utrillo at the Age of Two, 1886. Red chalk on paper, 10 3/4″ × 10 1/4″ (27 × 26 cm)
Musée National d'Art Moderne. Centre National d'Art et de Culture Georges Pompidou, Paris

PORTRAIT OF THE ARTIST, 1883. Pastel on paper, 17 3/4″ × 12 5/8″ (45 × 32 cm)
Musée National d'Art Moderne. Centre National d'Art et de Culture Georges Pompidou, Paris

in the town of Bessines, who presented to us a child of female sex, born that same day at six o'clock in the morning, in the house of Madame Guimbaud, widow, situated in the present town, to Madeleine VALADON, sewing maid, aged thirty-four, and to an unknown father +, residing in the town of BESSINES and to whom he stated he wished to give the first names MARIE CLEMENTINE.

The said declaration and presentation (were) made in the presence of Clément DOUY, aged forty-four, innkeeper, and Armand CHAZEAUD, blacksmith, aged forty, neighbors of the child, residing separately in the town of BESSINES, and the informant and the witnesses have signed with Us the present birth certificate, it having been duly read through.
+ The said Madeleine VALADON (signatures).»

It is thus quite certain that Suzanne Valadon came from a poor rural background. Brought up with no father by a mother who was a sewing maid, her social status would have an impact on her behavior and her work. There is one rather surprising anomaly: the identity card dated October 26, 1931, in the name of Madame Utter, known as Suzanne Valadon, states that she was born at Bessines on July 23, 1867, instead of September 23, 1865.

Why did she alter the month and the year? Did she wish to conceal her age out of feminine vanity, or was she seeking to avoid the implications of astrology, like Max Jacob, who used to say he was born on July 11 rather than 12 – an ill-omened day according to his horoscope? It is also quite possible that Suzanne's mother, a peasant with a poor memory and not much concern for the truth, had simply given her the wrong information. But does not the subterfuge in fact express a dissatisfaction with her birth as recorded by the authorities, a need to assert herself in a different way as proof of her own existence – by altering the facts, changing her first name and seeking to become another person?

Who was it that she finally succeeded in becoming? It is time to look for her real identity.

With her head filled with the novels of the day, Suzanne would claim to be the daughter of an aristocrat, a banker or a convict, while sometimes she said she had been abandoned by an irresponsible mother on the porch of Limoges Cathedral. Marie-Clémentine, who would later call herself Suzanne, told many different stories, but each time they contained a new version of her birth. Because she did not know who her father was, she invented a whole series of fathers, old and young, rich and poor – one thing she did not lack was imagination. But she suffered from a deep emotional maladjustment, an immense frustration which was to have an impact on her relationships with other people. In «Suzanne Valadon on the Absolute,» she writes: «The purpose of my life: equilibrium.» Only her art was to bring her a little of the serenity she sought so hard to find.

André Utter tried without success to write: «A life of Suzanne Valadon.» And yet he had noted a large number of events, collected documents and carried out a painstaking inquiry among his wife's family and friends. In the archives of the Musée National d'Art Moderne in Paris I was able to see his notes, as well as some precious letters and objects found in the artist's studio after her death. They had been bequeathed by Dr. Le Masle, a friend not only to Suzanne but also to Satie, Ravel, Cocteau and Marie Laurencin.

One page written by Utter describes the adventures of a certain Coulaud, the husband of his mother-in-law, Madeleine Valadon. He had apparently been convicted of forgery and sentenced to penal servitude by the Limoges criminal court. Madeleine, believing herself dishonored, left Bessines for Saint-Sulpice Laurière under her maiden name. She was employed as a servant in an inn, and this was probably where she met an engineer in charge of work on the Paris-Orléans railway in the Limoges area. Marie-Clémentine was the result of their romance, but she was never recognized by her father.

During the Second Empire, the flourishing building industry attracted a great many laborers from Limoges – bricklayers, chimney sweeps and carpenters – who went up to Paris to look for work. Madeleine Valadon, aged forty, joined the exodus and arrived in Montmartre with her small daughter, who had just turned five.

SELF-PORTRAIT, 1893. Oil on canvas, 15 3/4″ × 10 1/4″ (40 × 26 cm)
Collection: Jean Claude Bellier, Paris

MONTMARTRE, MY BEAUTIFUL VILLAGE

In about 1870, Marie-Clémentine discovered a village perched on a hill as green as her native countryside. Sheep and cows grazed beneath the sails of the windmills. Farmyards were alive with chickens, rabbits and pigs, and liquid manure flowed in the gutters in the middle of the lanes. Vines grew right up to the rue Cortot, alongside orchards full of fruit trees. The gardens were bright with wisteria, roses and lilac. As can be seen from the paintings by Georges Michel at the beginning of the century, Montmartre had all the charm of a country village, with its picturesque little streets winding up to the top of the Butte.

Madeleine Valadon went to live in a large working-class building in the boulevard Rochechouart. While she was out cleaning houses, Marie-Clémentine went to a convent school where she learned the fables of La Fontaine. She could still recite them at the end of her life.

Her excellent memory and love of poetry might have enhanced her gifts as an artist, but she had to leave school at the age of eleven in order to become an apprentice. It was not long before her manual dexterity was discovered. For a time she was employed in a milliner's workshop, where she decorated hats with feathers, flowers and birds, as well as embroidering coiffes. Later she worked in a factory making funeral wreaths, besides selling vegetables at Les Halles and becoming a waitress in a restaurant.

At the age of fifteen she was already familiar with the Montmartre of the artists. In 1881, quite close to her home, the Chat Noir cabaret, founded by Rodolphe Salis, opened at 84 boulevard Rochechouart beside the Elysée Montmartre dance hall. Just opposite Fernando had erected the big top of his circus, where Forain, Toulouse-Lautrec and Degas came to choose their models from among the acrobats, equestriennes and clowns.

The young Marie-Clémentine longed to join the circus. She dreamed of becoming a trapeze artist, but how could she get into such an unfamiliar world? One day her wish was fulfilled when she met at the Auberge du Clou, on the avenue Trudaine, two Symbolist painters, both of them Rosicrucians, Count Antoine de la Rochefoucauld and Théo Wagner, who later decorated the circus belonging to Médrano, Fernando's successor.

Marie-Clémentine's new friends took her to the Mollier circus, a private establishment at 8 rue de Bénouville in the 16th arrondissement. It was extremely fashionable at the time, frequented by circus lovers, actors and society people. On gala evenings Lautrec would meet his friends there, among them the photographer Sescau, who was employed as a mime and banjo player. Probably it was at the Mollier circus that Berthe Morisot drew the pretty Marie-Clémentine as a tightrope dancer, in a delicate, serene portrait which is a far cry from the real character of the high-spirited working-class girl.

Théo Wagner practiced riding while Marie-Clémentine, supple and muscular, performed feats on the big trapeze. Inexperienced, but hopelessly intrepid, she insisted on attempting somersaults although these had been strictly forbidden. One day she had a bad fall and seriously injured herself. It was the end of acrobatics and dreams of a life in the circus. Her exploits had been part daredevilry and part sense of physical achievement in the intoxicating feeling of flying through the air. She would have to find another way of realizing her ambitions.

The young people of the district used to congregate in the Moulin de la Galette dance hall: milliner's apprentices, models, shop assistants and the art students whom Roland Dorgelès described as «unkempt creatures with flapping trousers, long hair and a notion in their tiny brain that the artist's life consists of nothing but strolling about on the Butte.» Marie-Clémentine caused a sensation when she slid down the Moulin banisters like a tomboy.

Another favorite haunt was the Lapin Agile, a few yards away in the rue Saint-Vincent. The restaurant was still called Ma Campagne but already bore the sign, painted by the cartoonist André Gill, of a rabbit wearing a cap and jumping out of a saucepan. At Père Frédé's cabaret, Marie-Clémentine discovered the picturesque world of painters, poets and singers from the Chat Noir, among them a certain Boissy, who worked as an actuary in the «Abeille» insurance company. Was he the father of Maurice Utrillo, this curious character, frequenter of pubs and

The Tub, 1903. Distemper painting and pastel, 12 3/16″ × 11 3/8″ (31 × 29 cm)
Musées Nationaux, France. Bequest Pierre Lévy

After the Bath, 1908. Pastel, 20 3/8″ × 25 3/16″ (52 × 64 cm)
Collection: Oscar Ghez, Geneva

Young Girl Putting on a Stocking, c. 1896. Pastel, 12 3/8" × 8 1/8" (31.5 × 20.5 cm)
Private collection

YOUNG GIRL DOING CROCHET WORK, 1892. Oil on canvas, 18″ × 14 15/16″ (46 × 38 cm)
Musée National d'Art Moderne. Centre National d'Art et de Culture Georges Pompidou, Paris

FLOWERS, c. 1930. Oil on canvas. Private collection.

Still Life with Bouquet of Flowers, 1924. Oil on canvas, 31 1/2″ × 23 5/8″ (80 × 60 cm)
Musée d'Art Moderne de la Ville de Paris

Cat on Pink Drape, 1920. Oil on cardboard, 28 3/4″ × 21 1/4″ (73 × 54 cm). Private collection

occasional journalist and painter? Utrillo's biographer André Tabarant says that he was, but so many people have claimed the honor that it is much more likely his easygoing mother did not know herself which of her many lovers had given her a child. When the question was put to her by the painter and writer Jean Vertex, she replied, «It is difficult for me to tell you, because I really haven't the slightest idea.»

In 1883, Marie-Clémentine and her mother left the boulevard Rochechouart for 3 rue du Poteau, some distance from the center of Montmartre. At the foot of the Butte, on the Clignancourt side, there were still the old fortifications, and the area of low houses separated by market gardens as painted by Steinlen, with its poverty-stricken population of layabouts and street urchins, and the low bars described by Zola. The exuberant Marie-Clémentine did not like the gloomy district, which only brightened up in the spring when the trees burst into blossom.

It was there in a modest apartment, on December 26, 1883, that Maurice Valadon was born to Marie-Clémentine and an unknown father. To celebrate the event, Boissy offered drinks all around at the Lapin Agile, but he did not acknowledge the child. Marie-Clémentine's mother was left to look after the baby, while she herself, free and unmarried, earned her living as a model at the top of the hill.

My Utrillo at the Age of Nine, c. 1892. Black crayon, 9" × 11 13/16" (23 × 30 cm). Private collection

Still Life with Fruit Bowl, 1918. Oil on cardboard,
15 1/8″ × 20 7/8″ (38.5 × 53 cm)
Private collection

GLASSES ON A TABLE, 1917. Oil on canvas, 18 1/16″ × 21 5/8″ (46 × 55 cm)
Private collection

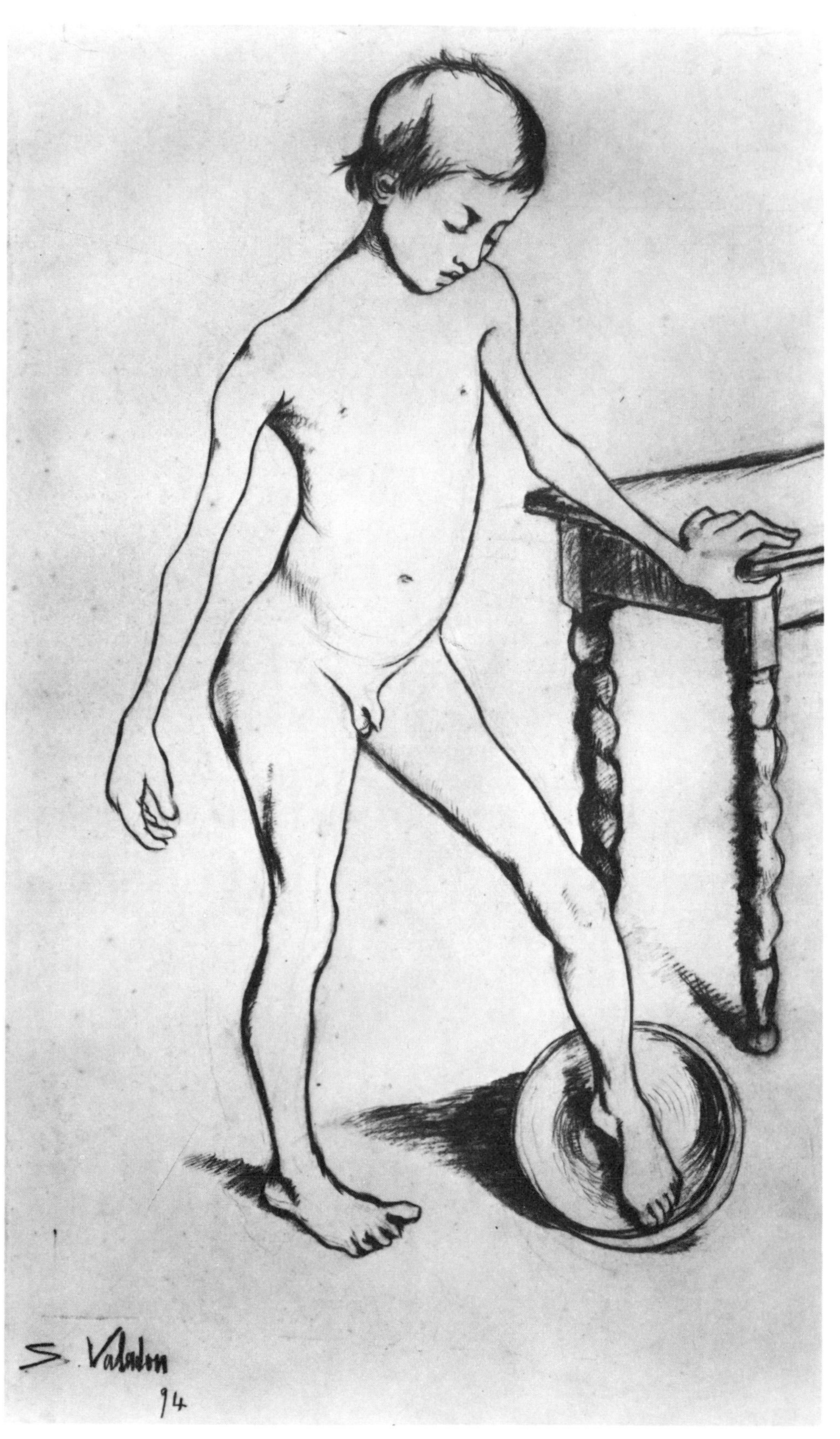

Utrillo Nude Standing Playing with a Wash Basin with His Foot, 1894
Drawing, 16 1/8" × 9 1/8" (41 × 23 cm)
Private collection

Woman Looking at Herself in the Mirror, 1920. Pastel, 17″ × 12 3/16″ (43 × 31 cm)
Private collection, Paris

NUDE AT THE MIRROR, 1909. Oil on canvas, 29 1/2″ × 36″ (90 × 71 cm)
Collection: F. Peter Model, New York

NEITHER WHITE NOR BLACK, 1909. Oil on cardboard, 39 3/4″ × 32 5/16″ (101 × 82 cm)
Musée National d'Art Moderne. Centre National d'Art et de Culture Georges Pompidou, Paris

Grandmother and Grandson, 1910. Oil on cardboard, 27 1/2″ × 19 5/8″ (70 × 50 cm)
Musée National d'Art Moderne. Centre National d'Art et de Culture Georges Pompidou, Paris

Sketch for Family Portrait, 1913. Black crayon, 31 1/2" × 24" (80 × 61 cm)
Private collection

Maria, as she was nicknamed by the painters, resembled the typical Montmartre girl described by Willette: sturdy and plump and bursting with health, graceful and seductive, an openhanded street arab, always smiling and showing off, lighthearted and sensual – and not in the least depraved. At the same time this unsettled orphan had an extraordinary need for affection. She, who had just given birth to a fatherless child, was always seeking a father. With her pretty laughing face, sparkling eyes and forthright way of speaking, she attracted the attention of painters and was always willing to pose for them.

THE «FAMOUS» MARIA

At the end of the last century the models used to parade every Sunday in the place Pigalle, where artists would come to select the virgins, muses, nymphs and goddesses they needed for the allegories of their academic painting.

Was Marie-Clémentine among the Italians and good-looking local girls who offered their services as models to both official painters and students from the Ecole des Beaux-Arts in search of sitters? Her contradictory statements throw little light on the story of her encounters with painters. Intuitively, perhaps, she was drawn toward talented artists, but it was more likely they who sought her out, attracted by her young beauty and vitality.

As a model, her career was outstanding. The famous artists who painted her portrait include Puvis de Chavannes, Renoir, Toulouse-Lautrec, Steinlen, Forain, the American Howland, de Nittis, and Princess Mathilde – first cousin of Napoleon III – who entertained the Goncourt brothers, Flaubert and Turgenev at her salon in the rue de Courcelles.

Henner, a Rome Prize winner who had become excessively conventional, finding ideal beauty in pale nudes and redheaded women, made Maria pose for four hours at a stretch for a whole fortnight, complimenting her at the end of the sittings on her physical endurance and intelligent approach. Wertheimer saw her as a sea nymph that he painted beside a sailor in *The Kiss of the Sea Nymph*, while the Czech Inaïs showed her as *Truth Emerging from the Well.*

Maria posed for one subject after another like an actress playing different parts. She was made use of. Created anew each time, she still had no existence of her own. She was a model, but one who was constantly being modeled; and, given her personality and temperament, it is easy to imagine the inner conflicts caused in the girl of fifteen by the continual change of identity required by the old gentlemen who painted her. Her feelings must certainly have been violent.

Was it Puvis de Chavannes who first noticed in the rue Lepic the mischievous girl who made mock of his affected manner? Did she go to his studio in the place Pigalle to deliver laundry washed by her mother? It is of little importance, but the meeting marked the beginning of a new life. For seven years, from 1880 to 1887, Maria was the perfect muse for *The Sacred Grove* and other paintings.

At the age of fifty-eight, Puvis was already a famous man, officer of the Legion of Honor (he would be made a commander four years later) and founder of the Salon des Artistes Français. His self-portrait shows that he must have been a reassuring figure, tall and solidly built, with his courteous manner, forceful features, clear gaze, and the nose he himself described as colossal. He detested the traditional image of the disorderly artist. Suzanne Valadon remembered him as a charming man: «He was always talking; quietly, slowly, but incessantly chatting about one thing and another. He was as curious as a woman. I would walk beside him and listen without saying a word. In any case I should not have known what to say to him. I was very much in awe of him . . . »

In the evening they would both return to Montmartre by bus. Puvis lived in the place Pigalle but worked in a studio at Neuilly near where his friend Seurat, who helped him prepare his huge compositions, was painting his famous picture *A Sunday Afternoon on the Island of La Grande Jatte.*

It took Puvis three years to complete *The Sacred Grove of the Muses,* a monumental work commissioned for the Palais des Arts in Lyons. Thirty years later his model was inspired

Miquel Utrillo Smoking a Pipe, 1891. Drawing, 6 7/8" × 4 3/8" (17.5 × 11 cm). Private collection

by the picture in her *Casting of the Net,** but the style was no longer symbolic. Where is Maria in *The Sacred Grove,* an imaginary landscape thronged with draped women? Is it her face that has been given to Architecture seated on a broken column, or Sculpture standing beside her, or Painting receiving the homage of a child who scatters flowers on her white dress? Is she Polyhymnia with her arm upstretched, Clio holding the writing tablets, Calliope reading, Thalia and Terpsichore listening to Erato and Euterpe, Urania contemplating the lake or Melpomene meditating beneath a willow? Maria is everywhere at once.

«I am there and again there,» she said to the art historian André Tabarant, who showed her a reproduction of the picture. «Almost all the figures have got something of me in them. I posed not only for the women but also for the young men. I am the ephebe plucking a branch from the tree, and he has my arms and my legs. Puvis would ask me to provide an attitude, a movement or gesture. He transposed and idealized.»

Recalling her youth, Suzanne Valadon said: «I was obsessed, a silly child who thought too much. I was a devil, I was like a boy.» Perhaps her masculine characteristics originated in the emptiness left in her life by the absence of a father. Is it not this complementary male side that Puvis discovered when he made her pose as a youth?

Apparently the relationship between the painter of *The Sacred Grove* and the little nymph who was forty-one years his junior, was that of father and daughter. Maria's need for affection was probably the reason she found some kind of compensation in seeking out elderly patrons. But there can be no doubt about the liaison between the artist, a *bon vivant* in spite of his respectable appearance, and his model. She was in love with him, an ambiguous feeling which, whether consciously or not, certainly had something incestuous about it. Suzanne Valadon never referred to the subject. She spoke only of the peaceful hours spent in the big studio at Neuilly, the visit of Princess Marie Cantacuzène, with whom Puvis was very much in love and who inspired a great deal of his work, and the generosity of the artist. Puvis had suggested giving her an allowance to enable her to bring up her son. Why did she not accept? Probably because she always insisted on being independent.

Utter states that he found a deed executed by a notary in which Puvis undertook to pay a sum of two hundred francs a year to Suzanne Valadon, but as he had torn it up, he was unable to provide any proof. The painter's will contains no mention of a legacy to his model, and Mr. René Puvis de Chavannes has affirmed that if his great uncle had believed himself to be the father of Maurice Utrillo, he would have left him as much money as he did his legitimate heirs.

In 1883, Puvis de Chavannes introduced Maria to Auguste Renior, who was looking for a model for his panels of *The Dance.* They liked each other at once: the painter of the *Moulin de la Galette* was born at Limoges near Bessines, and that was something they had in common. He was forty-two and Maria eighteen. Had she found yet another father?

«How many times I posed for heads for Renoir in one of his studios in the rue Saint-Georges or the rue d'Orchampt! I am the dancer who smiles as she falls into the arms of her partner, and I too am the fashionable young lady in long gloves and a dress with a train. At rue d'Orchampt I also sat for a scene at Bougival. As for the nudes, Renoir painted several from me, not only in a garden in the rue de la Barre which he had rented and where there was a shed which could be used as a shelter, but also in the studio in the boulevard de Clichy, for one of his pictures of bathers.» She posed outside, protected from prying eyes by the thick green of the bushes.

Heuzé claims that Aline Charigot, whom Renoir later married, did not approve of the constant presence of the attractive Maria. In a fit of jealousy she apparently rubbed out the face of her rival in *The Dance in the Country.* Renoir had to start the picture again with Aline as model. This may explain the uncertainty as to the identity of the woman in the painting. Suzanne Valadon never said much about the incident . . . and still less about a sitting when Aline found her in the painter's arms.

---

*See pp. 42-43.

PORTRAIT OF ERIK SATIE
1892-93
Oil on canvas
16 1/8″ × 8 5/8″ (41 × 22 cm)
Musée National d'Art
Moderne, Centre National
d'Art et de Culture
Georges Pompidou, Paris

A Nude Girl Reclining on a Couch, 1894
Black crayon on yellow tracing paper, 7 5/8" × 8 7/8" (19.4 × 22.6 cm)
Fogg Art Museum, Harvard University, Cambridge, Massachusetts. Bequest Meta and Paul J. Sachs

Driven out as an intruder, Maria began to pose frequently for Zandomeneghi, a Venetian Impressionist belonging to the Macchiaioli group, who was twenty-four years older than she was. He painted her portrait sitting at a table in the Nouvelle Athènes. This Montmartre brasserie in the place Pigalle had replaced the Guerbois as the Impressionists' favorite café. Here Jules Manet celebrated his Legion of Honor, and Degas, sitting at a crowded table, drew a profile of his friend Desboutin. Here too the Postimpressionists, Seurat, Signac and Pissarro, would rub shoulders with Gauguin, Guillaumin, Toulouse-Lautrec and Cézanne.

When Maria wanted to leave the rue du Poteau, Zandomeneghi found her an apartment on the first floor of his building, 7 rue Tourlaque, at the corner of the rue Caulaincourt. The house was full of artists. Renoir would share his models with Zandomeneghi, and on the third floor lived François Gauzi, a painter from Toulouse, who had recently been joined by his friend Toulouse-Lautrec.

The Little Girl Nude Seated on the Ground, Legs Outstretched, 1894
Drawing, 8 5/8" × 11" (22 × 28 cm)
Musée National d'Art Moderne. Centre National d'Art et de Culture Georges Pompidou, Paris

ADAM AND EVE, 1909. Oil on canvas, 63 3/4″ × 51 5/8″ (162 × 131 cm)
Musée National d'Art Moderne. Centre National d'Art et de Culture Georges Pompidou, Paris

Knowing that the newcomer was looking for a model to pose as an equestrienne, Zandomeneghi introduced him to his neighbor, Maria, the young trapeze artist from the Mollier circus. Captivated by the intrepid little lady, only a year younger than he was, Lautrec made her the heroine of his picture *The Circus.* Maria is the rider standing on the saddle of a horse getting ready to jump through a paper-covered hoop held by a clown. In order to paint the huge canvas, Lautrec for once made use of his nine-foot stepladder and his enormous easel.

Maria was most impressed by what she found in the studio, which, according to Gauzi, «was certainly not the most beautiful studio in Paris. It was characterized by two features that in no way disturbed the painter: inextricable disorder and quantities of dust . . . If one wanted to sit down, one had a choice between the divan, two stools and two chairs; a metal café table was used to put things down on. The model's table was cluttered with portfolios containing drawings and paintings, newspapers, books, and tracing paper, not to mention two dumbbells and a cup-and-ball which (the artist) never touched. There were boxes used as reliquaries for Japanese curios; Lautrec was particularly fond of a miniature reproduction of a samurai's lacquered helmet that he liked to show off by spinning it around on the tip of his thumb like a hat on a stand.»

Opposite the window, Maria noticed an unframed picture parodying *The Sacred Grove* by Puvis de Chavannes. The students at the Cormon studio, Emile Bernard among them, had amused themselves by making a pastiche of the work that had so impressed visitors to the 1884 Salon by its flat colors, the outline separating the figures from the landscape, and the simplification of the drawing. What could be easier! In two afternoons they had completed a caricature, introducing into *The Sacred Grove* a number of art students under the eagle eye of a policeman. Lautrec, shown in the foreground turning his back on the muses in a burlesque attitude, had signed on behalf of all of them this practical joke, as much a compliment as a criticism.

«You who pose in the nude for old men,» Lautrec said to Maria, «you ought to be called Suzanne.» She promptly adopted the new name that appears for the first time on her pastel self-portrait of 1883. Her liaison with Toulouse-Lautrec lasted for about two years. Until 1888 Suzanne posed for him as dancer, errand girl, a laundress carrying a heavy basket through the streets of Paris, a girl combing her hair or *The Woman in the Black Gloves.*

She can be recognized in *The Drinker* or *Hangover,* slumped over a café table with a vacant expression. It was a picture admired by Van Gogh for its technique so like his own, when he came timidly to show his paintings in Lautrec's studio, where nobody even looked at them. Suzanne was shocked: «Painters, they are all swine!» She is also to be seen sitting on a bench in the garden of the Père Forest, with a boater on her head and dressed in the high-necked white blouse of the Moulin de la Galette dancers painted by Renoir. Lautrec shows her looking sad, no longer young, although she was only twenty at the time. With her absent gaze, tight lips, pointed chin, tense attitude, and virile air in spite of the frail shoulders, he sees her as she depicted herself in her first self-portrait. And yet in the same year, 1885, Renoir in *The Braid* paints her with full lips, a cloud of hair and swelling breasts. What a contrast between the somber and the voluptuous Suzanne! «But which am I?» she may have thought when confronted by two such different interpretations.

Lautrec was tender and affectionate, but also tyrannical and demanding. Suzanne, capricious and sly, both encouraged him and sought to escape. They were always quarreling because the painter was irritated by her frequent disappearances and lies.

One day Gauzi burst into Lautrec's studio in a panic: «Maria wants to kill herself!» In fact, she had pretended to commit suicide in order to persuade her lover to marry her. Rushing into Maria's apartment, he heard Madeleine Valadon saying to her daughter: «That was a brilliant thing to do. He will never come back. A lot of good you have done yourself.» Whereupon Maria replied: «I could not get him to marry me, I had to do something drastic.» Hurt by these words, Lautrec decided not to see his girl friend again. «On leaving me,» writes Gauzi, «he probably went back to his studio and lay down on the divan, lost and miserable, shaking with sobs.»

Why did such a healthy peasant girl want to marry the deformed aristocrat? Some people would reply that it was for his money, which would have given her security and provided for

Joy of Living, 1911. Oil on canvas, 48″ × 81″ (122.8 × 231.1 cm)
The Metropolitan Museum of Art. Bequest of Miss Adelaide Milton de Groot

suzanne Valadon 1911

the education of her son. But is it not more likely that she was attracted by the cripple's powerful personality and virility? Suzanne was not in the least put off by either Lautrec's appearance or his passionate temperament, his drinking and eccentric behavior. She herself had no more prejudices than the descendant of the counts of Toulouse. They were both sensualists and shared a love of reality that they expressed in their art. As Suzanne said: «You must have the courage to look the model in the face if you want to reach the soul.»

Lautrec also helped her with her education. Having had to leave school at an early age, she now tried to make up for lost time by reading the painter's difficult books: «Force and Matter» by Ludwig Büchner, «The Genealogy of Morals» by Nietzsche, as well as the poems of Jehan Rictus, Maurice Rollinat and Baudelaire. In spite of its unhappy ending, the period was a fruitful one for Suzanne. Lautrec had awakened her slumbering genius and made her aware of her gifts as a painter.

THE BIRTH OF A VOCATION

The many artists for whom Suzanne Valadon posed never suspected that the little model they were painting was secretly preparing to become an artist herself. She taught herself by watching their gestures and techniques, the way they built up a picture, worked out the composition and placed the figures. As a model she exposed herself to the painter's eye; as an artist it was she who scrutinized the painter. She watched how he transferred her appearance to the canvas, and learned how to take advantage of the special relationship between the observer and the observed.

Unknown to himself, Puvis de Chavannes was an excellent teacher. She listened carefully to everything he said about painting and art, later confessing: «I never dared tell him that I was trying to draw, I who, ever since I was nine, had been drawing on any piece of paper I could find, to the great despair of my mother.»

As a child, Marie-Clémentine used to look out of the window on the boulevard Rochechouart and observe the men walking past in their top hats even in the morning, the women wearing feathered hats and long skirts, and the yellow cabs pulled by white horses. She sketched everything she saw, using chalk to draw on the walls the silhouettes of the passers-by – much to the annoyance of her mother, who immediately tried to rub them out – or drawing portraits on the pavement of the place Vintimille with the aid of little bits of charcoal.

Suzanne Valadon never attended an academy. Self-taught, she was unfettered by tradition or influence. Drawing was her way of affirming her existence, and when she had finished playing all the roles required of her as a model, she would try to capture her own body and her own face, in an attempt to find an identity. If she had read Descartes, she might have thought: «I paint, therefore I am.»

By painting self-portraits,* she strengthened her personality. And by representing her family and friends, she satisfied her need to make contact with other people. «I paint people in order to get to know them,» she said. The keenness of her observation was probably due to the necessity of establishing a direct relationship with those around her, thus making up for the lack of affection she found so hard to bear, with no father and an overworked, exhausted mother who was very seldom at home.

Although Henner thought that Suzanne Valadon's painting was very bad, he liked to think that he had given her the idea of becoming an artist. Unfortunately his former model was not in the least interested in imitating such an academic master. As they watched her art develop, all Maria's patrons must have thought they were responsible for her talent, when in fact they had only helped to bring it out. One day when Maria was late for a sitting, Renoir went to collect her from the rue du Mont-Cenis and found her busy doing a portrait of herself. «You too, and you never told me?» he said admiringly. She was overjoyed by the compliment.

---

*See frontispiece and pp. 6, 7, 12.

APPLES AND PEAR, 1900. Oil on canvas, 7 3/4″ × 12 5/8″ (20 × 32 cm)
Collection: Jean Claude Bellier, Paris

1914

Casting of the Net
1914
Oil on canvas
79 1/4″ × 118 3/8″
(201 × 301 cm)
Musée National
d'Art Moderne
Centre National
d'Art et de Culture
Georges Pompidou
Paris

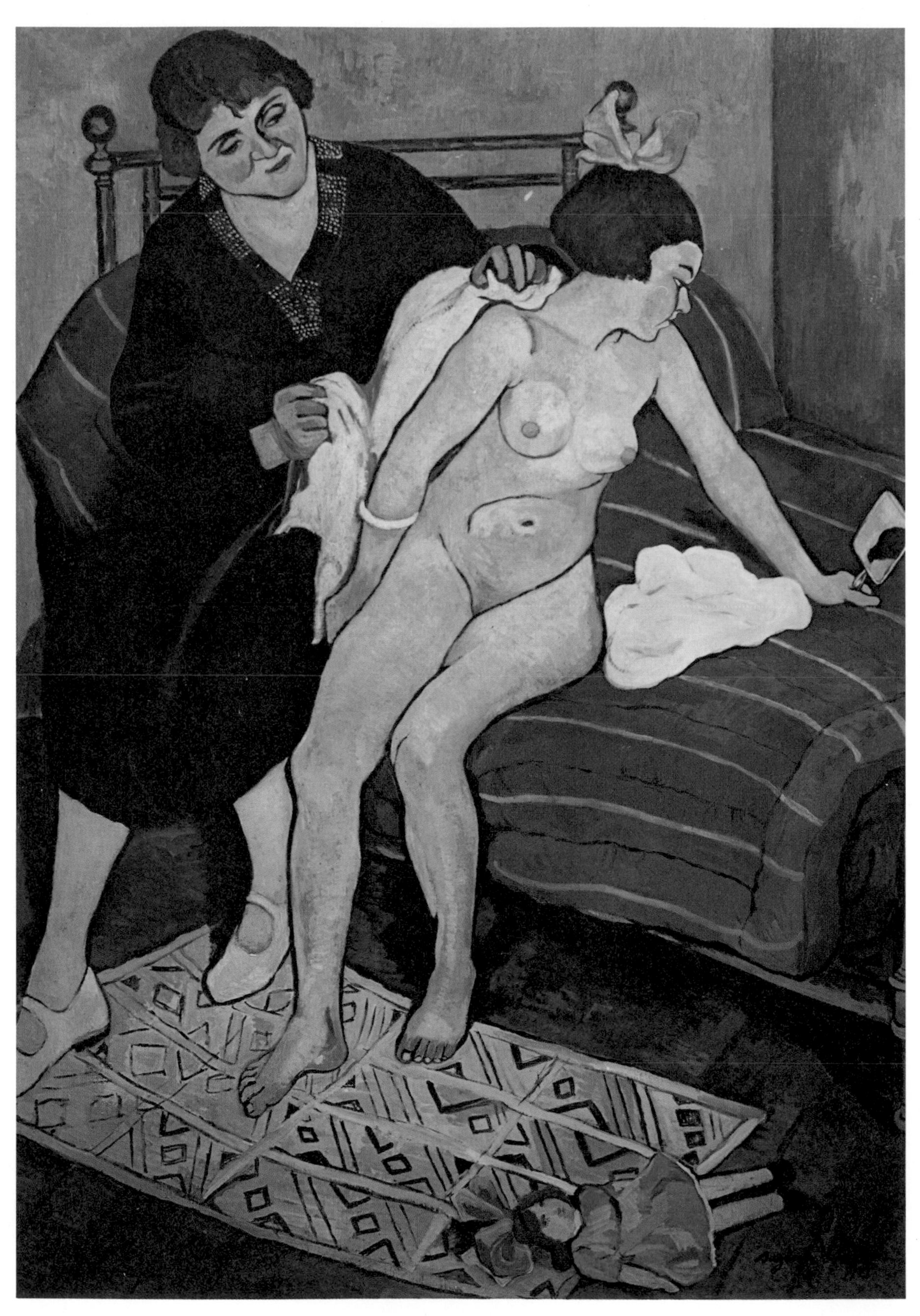

The Cast-Off Doll, 1921. Oil on canvas, 53 1/8″ × 37 3/8″ (135 × 95 cm). Private collection

Utrillo Nude Sitting on a Couch, 1895. Black crayon, 7 5/8" × 7 5/8" (19.5 × 19.5 cm)
Private collection

Maurice Utrillo Playing with a Sling-Shot, 1895. Black crayon, 7 1/2" × 13" (19 × 33 cm)
Private collection

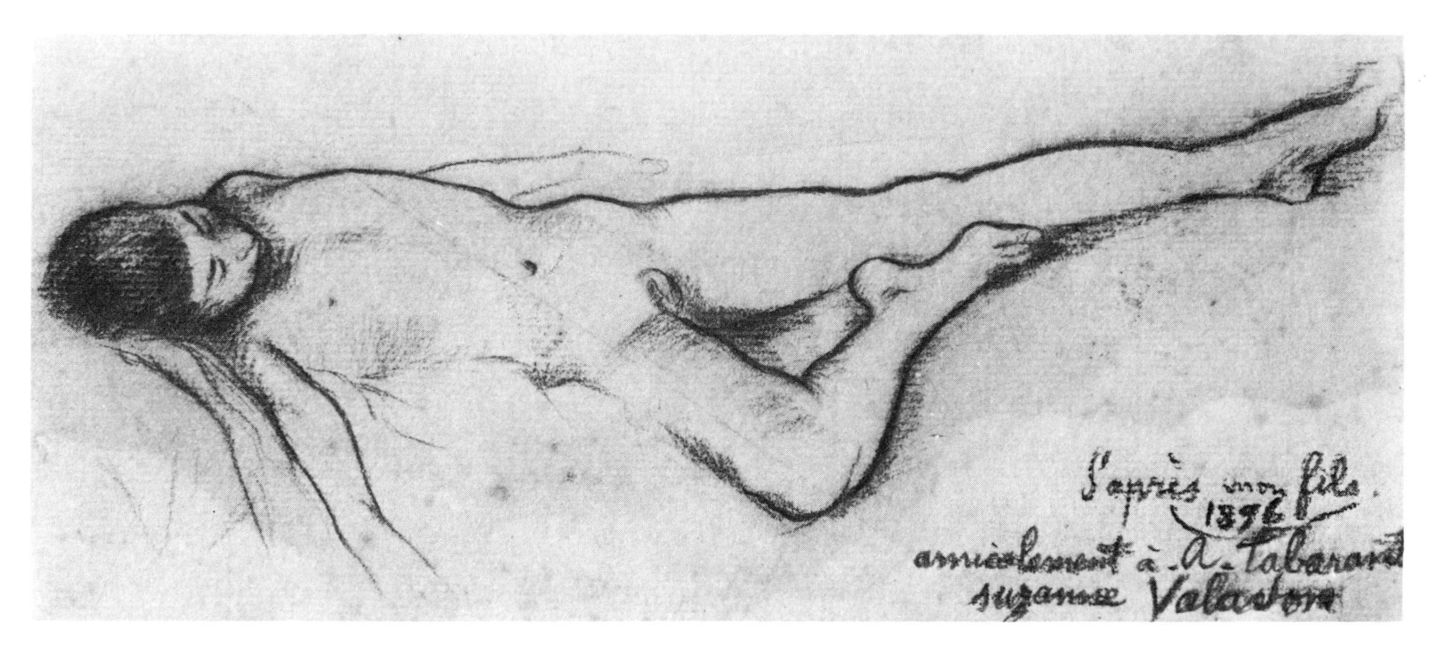

My Son, 1896. Black crayon, 4 1/8" × 9 7/16" (10.5 × 24 cm). Private collection

A comparison of Renoir's picture of Maria in *The Dance in Town* with this pastel self-portrait made in the same year, reveals a sharp contrast between Renoir's pretty, graceful, vivacious figure and her own scarcely flattering image of herself: unsociable, defiant, annoyed at not being able to express herself completely – although it is true the look on her face is softened by the bluish shades of the pastel.

«You have to be hard on yourself, be honest, and look yourself in the face,» said Suzanne Valadon. «You have to get rid of the surplus, the hatred and the excessive love.» Are not these words to be read on her proud adolescent face?

Suzanne attached great importance to the opinion of Lautrec, who had discovered by accident the drawings on the wall of her room. Astonished that she had done them herself, he selected a few of them to show to his friends. The first person he met was Gauzi:

«Look at this drawing, isn't it good?»

«Not bad – there is subtlety in the lines and sensitiveness in the approach! Who did it?»

«Maria – it is the portrait of her child, she knows how to observe and has got this far without taking lessons from anybody. Isn't it marvelous!»

«You must show it to Degas!» was the enthusiastic comment of the sculptor Bartholomé, who knew her well after doing a portrait of her in pastel.

Armed with a letter of introduction, Maria hesitantly approached Degas, an artist of extreme sensitivity but one who could also be merciless, unreasonable, quick-tempered and pessimistic. Certainly he did not believe in spontaneous talent but pinned his faith on traditional teaching.

Suzanne Valadon has described the interview: «Degas welcomed me very kindly and showered me with praise. From that day I became a firm friend. He hung one of my red chalk drawings in his dining room *(The Model Getting out of the Bath near an Armchair)*. I visited him every afternoon. I often met Bartholomé there, who was an inseparable friend, and also Rouart. If a few days passed without my going to see him, I was sure to be fetched by his housekeeper, the faithful Zoé . . . I never posed for him, although people are always saying that I did.»

THE WORK OF AN AUTODIDACT: DRAWING COMES FIRST

Paul Pétridès, the picture dealer, has drawn up a catalogue of almost all Suzanne Valadon's works: 276 paintings, 273 drawings, and 31 prints. She spent the ten years from 1883 to 1893 doing nothing but drawings. Both dates are marked by self-portraits,* one in pastel, austere, plastic, half in shadow, and the other a simple outline in pencil which she gave to Erik Satie in 1893, the year in which she finished the musician's portrait.

Her first models were her own family: her young son and her mother, her niece Marie Cola,** and the little Gilberte. Her style is pure and controlled, whether she is drawing a child's limbs or her mother's heavy features and lined face. In everyday life Suzanne appears undisciplined and inconsistent, but as an artist she is very different: rigorous, accurate, displaying total mastery of her art.

A possessive mother often dismayed by the task of bringing up a difficult little boy, she was thrilled as an artist when Maurice, the only person she ever really loved, consented to pose for as much as a few seconds at a time. At that point he belonged to her completely. Her lines become softer as she lovingly draws his face on the paper.

The romantic red chalk profile breathes a genuine tenderness. The two-year-old child might be any age. His long tousled hair and sad eyes are reminiscent of the portraits by Dürer that Suzanne admired so much, as well as the works of Cranach and other German masters of the sixteenth century.*** The same gracefulness is to be found in the face and gestures of *My Son at the Age of Seven* and *My Utrillo at the Age of Nine.*****

In 1891, Suzanne drew a portrait of Paul Mousis, the rich man she was to marry five years later. She also did a portrait of Miquel Utrillo y Molins, the generous Catalan who, on January 27, signed a legal recognition of paternity of Suzanne's illegitimate son. In profile, *Miquel Smoking a Pipe,****** with his fine features, lowered eyes and air of melancholy, shows many points of resemblance with Maurice. But that is scarcely sufficient proof that he was his father, as is increasingly believed today. Miquel never explained his action, but he probably believed himself to be the father and so considered it his duty to give his name to the child. His discretion, combined with the contradictory statements of Suzanne, allows absolutely no certainty as to the real father of Maurice.

What is known about the brief liaison? Miquel Utrillo's father belonged to a group of liberals, and was forced to go into exile in France with his family in 1868. Miquel himself studied agronomy, but was a frequent visitor to Montmartre where he liked to paint, often spending the night at the Moulin de la Galette. On one such occasion he met Suzanne Valadon and became her lover. According to the Barcelona writer, Enric Clarasso, they were constantly quarreling, which would explain Miquel's dedication on a drawing of Suzanne dated 1894: «In memory of the Seven Years' War.» They can be seen together on the Butte in paintings by Rusinol and Opisso. But Miquel spent most of his time in Spain. He was an architect, the founder of a review and master of ceremonies at the famous cabaret «ELS 4 Gats» in Barcelona, often visited by the young Pablo Picasso.

1894-1896 were years of intensive work for Valadon. Degas' encouragement was beginning to bear fruit. Undaunted by the difficulties involved, she drew a whole series of nudes standing, lying, squatting or sitting on the ground in contorted postures. In *Utrillo Standing Nude Playing with a Wash Basin with His Foot,******* Maurice appears at the age of eleven, slight, long-limbed, bending backward with outstretched arms, a broad hand at the end of a slender wrist leaning on the table to maintain his balance. The children Suzanne draws often have angular shoulders and hips, and protruding chests and ribs, whereas the adolescents and women are plump and well covered. The hard black line emphasizes the structure of their bodies.*******

---

* See pp. 10, 6. ** See p. 61. *** See p. 9. **** See p. 21. ***** See p. 31. ****** See p. 24. ******* See pp. 45, 46, 47, 50, 66, 74.

VASE OF FLOWERS ON A LOW WALL, 1920. Oil on canvas, 21 1/4″ × 18″ (54 × 46 cm)
Private collection

Utrillo Nude Standing and the Grandmother Sitting, 1894
Black crayon, 16 7/8" × 8 1/4"
(43 × 21 cm)
Private collection

Pierre Georgel, curator of the Dijon Museum, writes as follows: «I suggest that admirers of Balthus should turn their attention to the drawings of Suzanne Valadon around 1900. They cannot fail to recognize their bizarre quality, which is the more striking because it is not deliberate. What innocence or what perversity is to be found in *The Little Girl Nude Seated on the Ground.** Here is an original contribution to the imagery of the modern Eros, even if the formal composition is taken from Degas.» The remark could also apply to *A Nude Girl Reclining on a Couch*** in the Boston Museum, a real «Lolita» after Nabokov's heart.

Suzanne Valadon's figures are shown in the setting of her own apartment – in a simple dining room, kitchen or bedroom.

The grandmother or servants busy themselves around the bathtub (*Little Girl Nude and Servant*). An old woman holds a basin. Her shoulders strain under the weight of the water. She leans over to pick up the towels, bent in two as much by age as by the tiring nature of her task. The bath session fills the entire sheet of paper, an everyday scene here depicted as a dramatic event. In *Nude Getting into the Bath Beside the Seated Grandmother,* the bathtub, the water jug and – on the chest – the basin, the jug, the towel and the dressing gown, are given as much importance as the figures themselves. In another series of drawings, adolescent girls dry themselves (*After the Bath*), brush their hair (*Nude Standing Doing Her Hair*), pin up their long hair (*Woman Doing Her Hair*), wash their feet (*Young Girl Kneeling in a Tub*), get out of the tub (*The Bath*), or perform routine tasks in a modest bedroom. They show every part of their body without any shame, but with so much naturalness and simplicity that there is nothing really indecent in their attitudes.***

These are, of course, the subjects that Degas liked to paint, but the style is not the same. In «Les Etapes de la Peinture Contemporaine,» Bernard Dorival discusses the differences between the style of the master and that of his young protégée. Degas analyzes reality, while Suzanne, closer in this to Lautrec (*Young Girl Putting on a Stocking*),**** makes a synthesis of the real. «Whereas each one of Degas' lines corresponds with a need to know the form, to dissect the movement, to seize the mechanism of the gesture, Valadon only notices, only selects and only draws the lines that express the character of the models and help to give concrete form to the emotions which she herself felt when painting them.»

In 1894, Suzanne Valadon exhibited for the first time at the Salon de la Nationale. It was by no means easy. Puvis de Chavannes had at first discouraged her: «It's impossible. Whose pupil are you? What will people say?»

Disregarding his gloomy remarks, she went to visit Bartholomé. The sculptor, who had already introduced her to Degas, wrote to Paul Helleu, the president of the Salon: «My dear Helleu, four or five days ago there arrived at my house, sent by a friend, a poor woman carrying an enormous parcel of drawings. She wanted to exhibit at the Champ de Mars and was looking for someone to sponsor her. I do not recommend her to you, I only ask you to look at the drawings signed Valadon when they come before the selection committee. You will see that they have some serious defects, but I think they also have such unusual qualities that you will probably be glad to accept them . . . »

The selection committee allowed her to exhibit *The Toilet of the Grandson, Grandmother and Grandson,* and three studies of children. One study attracted attention, and an enlightened critic wrote several eulogistic pages on it. The press-cutting agency sent the article by mistake to Jules Valadon, the establishment painter. Furious, he instructed Suzanne to sign her first name in full rather than S. Valadon, as the S could be mistaken for a J.

Degas was the first to buy drawings from her – three of them. He introduced her to collectors and to Le Barc de Bouteville, who was the dealer for Lautrec, Emile Bernard, Sérusier, Pissarro, Cézanne and Gauguin. He also put her in touch with Durand-Ruel, Le Veel and Vollard, who were interested in her work.

---

* See p. 35. ** See p. 34. *** See pp. 75, 54, 59, 67. **** See p. 16.

TREE AT MONTMAGNY QUARRY, c. 1910. Oil on canvas,
21 1/4″ × 28 3/4″ (51.5 × 73 cm)
Museum of Art, Carnegie Institute, Pittsburgh, Pennsylvania

The Sacré-Cœur, Seen from the Garden of the Rue Cortot, 1916
Oil on canvas, 24 3/4″ × 20 7/8″ (63 × 53 cm)
Musée National d'Art Moderne. Centre National d'Art et de Culture Georges Pompidou, Paris

Woman Combing Her Hair, c. 1905. Drawing, 10 1/4" × 7 3/4" (25.7 × 19.7 cm)
Museum of Art, Carnegie Institute, Pittsburgh, Pennsylvania

At the same time Degas, who always encouraged the progress of this gifted novice, decided that etching would be good practice for her, and he taught her the technique of soft-ground etching. It was the only direct teaching she ever had. Suzanne used a pastel sketch of *Catherine in the Tub* to make her first etching in 1894, printed on her master's press.

Determined to do it all herself, she pressed so hard on the tool that she made a line in the zinc which came through the protective coating. Claude Roger-Marx analyzes her work as follows: «The artist has driven her line straight like a plowman; the acid seething in the furrows will enlarge them still further. Soft-ground etching technicians excel with grays, pale golds and halftones. Here it is almost as if a sculptor had defined the planes, contrived the profiles and given so much weight to each form, in particular to the nudes which, although produced on white paper, have the gloss and the hardness of marble.»

When she was etching Suzanne expended so much energy on her copper that she found in this creative act a new kind of fulfillment.

In 1895, Ambroise Vollard published the first plates by Suzanne Valadon in «Le Rêve et l'Idée» and «Album des Peintres graveurs.» But the irrepressible Maria was always on the lookout for new discoveries and decided to combine the technique of soft-ground etching with that of drypoint in *Louise Nude Does Her Hair.* Lastly she tackled conventional etching in 1904 in *Women and Children Beside the Water* which recalls her first nudes in the open air inspired by Puvis de Chavannes' *The Sacred Grove.*

Degas encouraged her to go on working, to make the most of her remarkable talent, and be more self-confident. Old and lonely, he was worried about his protégée and wrote to her in about 1900. «My dear Maria, your letter always reaches me punctually with its firm, copperplate handwriting. It is your drawings I do not see any more. From time to time in my dining-room (sic) I look at your red chalk drawing which still hangs there. And I say to myself: "That little devil Maria was a genius at drawing." Why do you no longer show me anything? I am nearly sixty-seven . . . » Maria was just thirty-five. Degas was obliged to leave his house in the rue Victor Massé as it was threatened with demolition. His friends wanted him to rent an apartment in Passy where he would have been bored stiff. Maria found him a studio in the boulevard de Clichy and spared him the sorrow of having to leave Montmartre.

To a questionnaire drawn up by Germain Bazin for his «Histoire de l'Art contemporain,» Suzanne Valadon replied without false modesty: «*Training:* Independent – innate talent, exceptionally gifted. *Principal stages of artistic life:* since 1883 when she began, has been drawing like a maniac, not in order to make beautiful drawings to be framed, but to do good drawings that capture an instant of life, full of movement and intensity.»

She also said: «I have been drawing madly so that when I no longer have any eyes, I shall have them in my fingertips.» Between 1896 and 1903 Suzanne Valadon was drawing less. She had decided to be a painter and in order to practice with color, she began by using pastel.*

1892: COLOR

«I painted at the age of fourteen, I painted with whatever I had, indiscriminately,» says Suzanne Valadon, but she also states: «I was so wild and proud that I did not want to paint.»

What explains this fear of progressing from drawing to painting? Drawing is a kind of writing, a projection of the artist; painting is a painstaking possession of the materials which must be made to live and move on their own. Color requires a technique which does not need lines. The young Suzanne was frightened by all the new difficulties to be overcome, not wanting to discover her own shortcomings when faced with an empty canvas. She mistrusted the «dirty and nauseating» pigments and found them complicated to manipulate. When she met Lautrec, however, Suzanne realized that she could become a painter. She learned a lot from him by observing

---

* See pp. 14, 15, 25.

GARDENS OF THE RUE CORTOT, 1922. Oil on canvas, 46 1/8″ × 35 7/16″ (117 × 90 cm)
Private collection

the large oval palette that he never cleaned, where the pigments were reduced to a minimum; or watching as he blocked out his canvas with colors thinned with turpentine, before getting down to the picture itself.

Suzanne's first paintings, *Portrait of a Little Girl, Young Girl Doing Crochet Work,** *Portrait of Erik Satie*** of 1892-1893, show her painting with a sure hand but without yet having discovered the style that would make her work so original. The portrait of Erik Satie reveals a nonviolent Expressionism with colors that are already those of the Fauves, and brush strokes in the form of bold streaks and hachures like the ones she admired in Toulouse-Lautrec and Van Gogh. The musician has a Bohemian air with his long hair, half-starved face, pince-nez, curled mustache, and battered hat.

When Satie posed for her, he was twenty-six and Suzanne twenty-seven. They had met at the Lapin Agile and the Auberge du Clou, where Satie earned his living by playing the piano, although this «father of modern music» had already attracted attention with his «Gymnopédies» and «Gnossiennes.» Suzanne went to visit him at 6 rue Cortot in a little attic room that he called his cupboard. It was the beginning of a new romance which lasted six months, from January to June 1893.

Satie's passion is revealed in a letter dated March 11, written with care in the form of a poem. The writing paper bears the blue embossed stamp of the «Société des Vieilles Poules» (Society of Old Hens) founded in 1881, complete with the motto «Eagle I cannot be, Turkey I scorn to be, Hen I am.» He writes with beseeching tenderness and his usual sense of humor: «Dear little Biqui, impossible to stop thinking about you and everything you are; you are totally within me, everywhere I see nothing but your exquisite eyes, your soft hands and your little childish feet. . . » He goes on to complain of the icy solitude that «leaves the head empty and the heart full of sadness» and suggests three rendezvous in the hope of meeting her at least once, for he was beginning to understand that she was not always able to do as she pleased.

In fact, Suzanne had fallen in love with somebody else. She had met Paul Mousis, a friend of Satie's, at the Lapin Agile. He was chief clerk at the firm of Bel et Sainbéant, and did not belong to the artists' world. Possibly she was attracted to him because he posed no threat to her own personality. She finally allowed herself to marry him on August 5, 1896. As a man of means he was able to provide for the material well-being of the family, and for fifteen years Suzanne led a comparatively peaceful and affluent life, working as she liked and even making furniture – chairs and armchairs of solid oak – using a saw, a file and a hammer. She spent her time between the comfortable house in the country at Pierrefitte where her mother and Maurice lived, and the studio Mousis had given her at 12 rue Cortot.

This venerable Montmartre dwelling had seen many famous people in the course of the centuries. It was built in the reign of Henry IV, not far from the lodge where *le vert galant* used to meet Gabrielle d'Estrée. In 1680, Claude de la Rose, better known as Rosimond, an actor in Molière's company, went to live in the small house at the bottom of the garden that is now the Montmartre museum.

It was at 12 rue Cortot in 1875 that Renoir painted the *Moulin de la Galette, Coming Out of the Conservatory,* and *The Swing.* He used to keep his canvases and easels in an old stable which was immediately underneath the studio where the Valadon-Mousis couple would live twenty years later. The house also owed its fame to a group of anarchists, as well as a number of other well-known artists and poets all of whom lived there at one time or another: the Post-impressionist painter Maximilien Luce, Emile Bernard, Raoul Dufy, Othon Friesz, Poulbot, Galanis, Léon Bloy, Pierre Reverdy, founder of the review "Nord-Sud," and Antoine, the director of the Théâtre Libre.

It took Suzanne forty minutes to reach the rue Cortot from Pierrefitte, driving in her mule-drawn tilbury. Her German shepherd dogs went with her. She was delighted to be able to

* See p. 17. **See p. 33.

Grandmother Holding the Wash Basin for a Young Girl, 1910
Black crayon, 9" × 8 5/8" (23 × 22 cm). Private collection

paint exactly as she pleased. Only one thing spoiled her happiness: her son was already showing the first symptoms of alcoholism. His grandmother encouraged him to drink for the sake of peace. Suzanne, on the advice of a doctor, taught Maurice to paint, and Paul Mousis found a job for him, as the boy was continually playing hooky from the Collège Rollin. But none of this had any effect, and Suzanne, who recognized Maurice's budding genius, shut her eyes to his drinking.

On January 1, 1896, the year of Suzanne's marriage to Mousis, Maurice, apparently at his grandmother's dictation, had written a despairing letter to Miquel Utrillo, complaining that Utrillo whom he believed to be his father, had abandoned him, and that he was neglected by his mother and Paul Mousis, who had sent him to boarding school. But for Suzanne herself, painting mattered more than anything. Her work is incontestably original – uncompromising, daring, passionate and never for one moment facile or superficial.

NUDES AND PORTRAITS

Between her first portraits, *Erik Satie, Young Girl Doing Crochet Work,* and her major composition of 1903, *The Moon and the Sun* or *The Brunette and the Blonde,* one of her earliest

Young Girl Kneeling in a Tub, c. 1910. Red chalk, 7 1/2" × 10 3/4" (19 × 27 cm). Private collection

pictures of nudes, Suzanne Valadon's style had changed. She had retained something of Puvis de Chavannes, and, without having known Gauguin, was influenced by him. She had often seen his pictures in the galleries of Vollard and Théo Van Gogh, and probably in Degas' home as well. Certainly she had visited the Café Volpini in 1889 where the exhibition of «Synthetist Impressionists» showed the pictures by the Pont-Aven group that had been rejected at the Salon of the World Fair. She had assimilated widely differing influences but without ever imitating a particular artist. Her painting always remained personal.

She sets her nudes in a decorative landscape complete with the laurel wreaths of which Puvis was so fond, or outlines her colors in black like Gauguin, or distorts the bodies with plunging perspectives like those in a Japanese print. And yet all these borrowings result in a work which is entirely original in its mixture of stylization and realism, truth and artifice – as if the realism were enhanced by the stylistic devices.

When her doctor friend Robert Le Masle asked her to explain the title of her picture *Neither White nor Black** of 1909, she replied that, according to the precepts of Renoir, pure white and black did not exist in painting. It was for this reason that she had begun to color her outlines. The picture may be compared with Picasso during his Ingres period. The unbroken, unhachured line obeys the rule of Ingres: «The simpler the lines and form, the more beauty and force they convey. Each time you divide up the forms, you weaken them.» The painter of *La Source* also said: «If I had to put a sign over my door, I would write "School of Drawing" and I am sure I would turn out painters!» The words might have been addressed to Suzanne Valadon.

There is a case to be made for comparing *Two Nudes* or *The Bath*** with Courbet's *Bathers*, but with Suzanne everything is drawn with precise lines, whereas Courbet's picture is all painting without any definite outlines.

Surely she was inspired by the Nabis and Matisse in decorative backgrounds like the arabesques of patterned materials in *The Blue Room**** in which space is made opaque by the hangings behind the figure. Like Matisse she abhors a vacuum. It is possible to find many other analogies between her paintings and those of artists from different epochs. But in her thoughts on art, Suzanne Valadon explains that she owes everything to herself: «I think that true theory is imposed by nature; in the first place the nature of the painter and secondly that of what he is representing. Has there ever been a painter, in the real sense of the word, who has painted as he wished? Everyone paints as he sees, which is the same thing as saying that everyone paints as he can.»

*Nude at the Mirror***** of 1909 has the same subject as the many drawings of women at their toilet she worked on with so much care, but here, because of the color, the setting assumes a totally different importance – the vase of flowers on the table, the pictures on the wall and, in the background, the room with its patterned wallpaper. The painting marks a new departure: an intimate relationship between figure and setting.

In an article in the «Intransigeant» on the Salon des Indépendants of 1911, Guillaume Apollinaire describes her nudes as «disillusioned.» They are usually heavy, sturdy, composed in broad masses.

As André Warnod writes: «The black outline of the nudes makes the contours clear but leaves intact the touching sensitiveness of the flesh, flesh which is sometimes soft and sometimes slack. The pitiless line, precise and firm, may emphasize the defects, the wrinkles in the belly, the sagging breasts – a good drawing is not always a pretty one – but the flesh is always alive and beautiful because of the life that breathes through it, fresh because of the blood that can be felt flowing beneath the skin. The nudes she paints with such a clear and radiant palette are enchanting because of the truth that emanates from them, nudes full of strength and

---

* See p. 27. ** See p. 82. *** See p. 77. **** See p. 26.

MARIE COLA AND HER DAUGHTER GILBERTE, 1913. Oil on canvas, 63 3/8″ × 51 1/8″ (161 × 130 cm)
Musée de Lyon, France

Portrait of Monsieur Mori, 1922. Oil on canvas, 23 5/8″ × 22 7/16″ (68 × 57 cm)
Musée de Menton, France

Portrait of Madame Coquiot, 1915. Oil on canvas, 36 5/8″ × 28 3/4″ (93 × 73 cm)
Musée de Menton, France

Maurice Utrillo at His Easel, 1919. Oil on canvas, 18 7/8″ × 17 3/4″ (48 × 45 cm)
Musée d'Art Moderne de la Ville de Paris

movement, and also nudes lying on a divan. What sensual power is evoked by the broad hips and smooth belly, by this woman who offers herself and lies waiting!»

The male-female ambiguity that can be detected in the artist's character, and which emerges in her art, does not escape the poet and critic Francis Carco: «The nude figures of Madame Suzanne Valadon strike a quite exact balance between the rigor of a masculine vision and that something which, out of an intention that is pitilessly equal, but from an obscurely defensive instinct, is deliberately left to the feminine touch . . . The line becomes more human. And here it is apparent that Madame Suzanne Valadon is a woman . . . The art of today can look upon her as the most realistic woman painter of the nude.» Later he mentions the unconscious narcissism which is one of the dominant features of the painter's character.

Suzanne Valadon's extensive output after 1909 was due to her meeting with one of her son's friends, André Utter, who was to change her whole life. She first noticed the young man one evening when he brought Maurice home in a sadly drunken condition. She saw him again at Montmartre, busy at his easel, and called out as she hurried on with her two large dogs, «You can't paint the sky in the same way as the earth!»

Utter described the scene to André Warnod: «She had amazing light eyes, and black hair parted down the middle, and she seemed to dance rather than walk. She had something of both an Amazon and a fairy . . . »

The young artist was an electrician, the son of a plumber in the rue Ramey, who liked to visit the Butte in order to satisfy his passion for painting. A few days later Suzanne saw him from her window in the rue Cortot and asked him to come up to her studio, where she suggested that he should pose in the nude for Adam in a large composition. The twenty-four-year-old Adam helped Suzanne, who was well into her forties, to recover something of the passion of her youth, while she initiated Utter into a hitherto unknown world of sensuality.

Suzanne began frenziedly painting *Adam and Eve,** a canvas measuring 1 meter 61 centimeters, at once decorative, allegorical and realistic. It shows herself and Utter in the idealized landscape of the Garden of Eden, as a symbol of their love for one another.

The same year Suzanne left the rue Cortot and went to live for a few months with Utter, Utrillo, her mother and the dogs, at 5 impasse Guelma, a building already inhabited by Braque, Dufy and Severini. She had finally left Paul Mousis, who could no longer stand the impossible behavior of the family and Maurice's constant drinking. It was not long before they were divorced. The «tribe» returned to 12 rue Cortot when Emile Bernard vacated his studio up in the attic. This pioneer of the Pont-Aven group had written over his door: «Let him who does not believe in God, Raphael and Titian not enter here!» The «accursed threesome» disobeyed the commandment and walked in.

I have seen this apartment, at present occupied by Madame Vertex. The wooden staircase, the heap of coal on the landing, the barking of the dog on the other side of the door – nothing seemed to have changed. On the right of the entrance was the little room looking onto the rue Cortot where Utrillo would shut himself in to paint his view of Paris from postcards; and to the left was the big studio lit by a huge skylight giving onto the gardens of the museum. It was their «central laboratory,» as Max Jacob would have said.

They each worked independently, constantly hurling abuse at one another, usually for the most trivial reasons: a tube of zinc white that had disappeared, a dirty paintbrush, or a jar of turpentine with paint in it. The atmosphere was tense between the strong-willed Suzanne, the lover she married in 1914 and Maurice, shocked and jealous, badly behaved and unloved, who would come home between drinking bouts to be forgiven if he brought back a masterpiece. Suzanne would always give in when confronted with her son's success as a painter, even if he

---

* See p. 36.

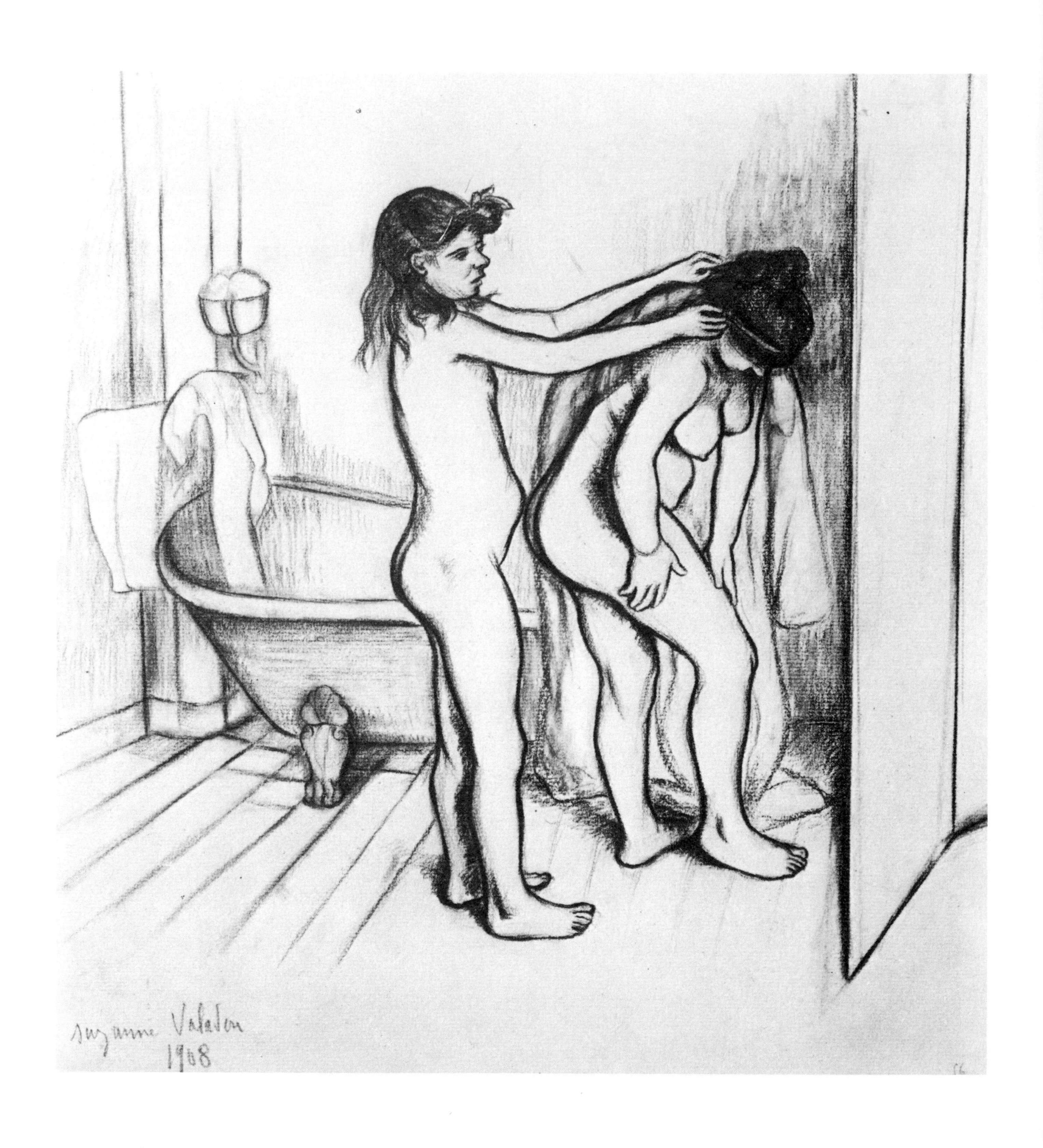

Mother and Daughter after the Bath, 1908
Crayon and pastel, 12" × 11" (30.5 × 28 cm). Private collection

The Bath, 1908. Crayon and pastel, 11 3/4" × 12 3/4" (30 × 32.5 cm)
The Detroit Institute of Arts. John S. Newberry Bequest

Still Life with a Teapot, 1911. Drawing, 15 3/8" × 22 1/16" (39 × 56 cm)
Musée National d'Art Moderne. Centre National d'Art et de Culture Georges Pompidou, Paris

was pursued by the police or discovered lying dead drunk with his clothes torn to shreds on the sidewalks of the Butte. In fact, the trio lived mainly on the proceeds of his paintings, which were sold for him by Utter.

At the same time as the nudes, Suzanne Valadon began a series of group portraits in 1910. *Grandmother and Grandson** adds a new dimension to her art with the primitive awkwardness in the arrangement of the figures, in particular their faces and hands, set against a background of flowers without any depth. In this work, stripped to essentials, the inner life of the models is rendered by the accuracy of the drawing: Maurice appears dreamy, his grandmother resigned and the dog full of confidence. Once again Suzanne has succeeded in reconciling the rigor of an artificial composition with a true portrayal of the characters which she obtains more by the keenness of her observation than by any psychological insight. In *Family Portrait*** (1912), Suzanne appears standing with one hand on her bosom, taking her rightful place in the center of the group.

She scrutinizes her models with merciless acuity: they are shown quite simply as

* See p. 28. ** See p. 29. *** See p. 70.

Still Life with a Violin Case, 1923. Oil on canvas, 31 7/8″ × 39 3/8″ (81 × 100 cm)
Musée d'Art Moderne de la Ville de Paris

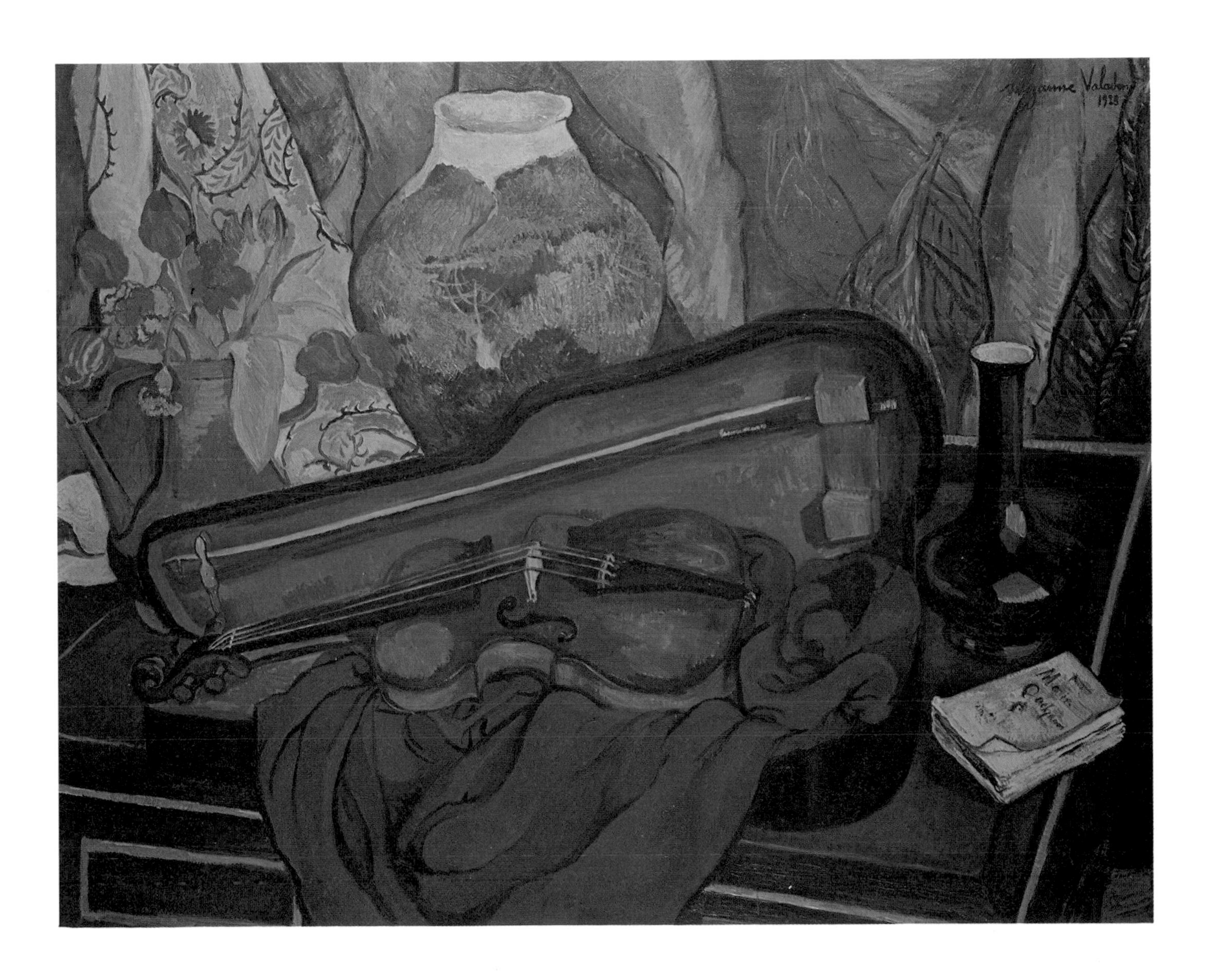

Portrait of Miss Lily Walton, 1922. Oil on canvas, 39 3/8″ × 31 7/8″ (100 × 81 cm)
Musée National d'Art Moderne. Centre National d'Art et de Culture Georges Pompidou, Paris

STILL LIFE WITH DUCK, 1930. Oil on canvas, 28 3/4″ × 23 5/8″ (73 × 60 cm)
Musée de Besançon, France

PORTRAIT OF A WOMAN, 1921. Oil on canvas, 16 7/8″ × 19 5/8″ (43 × 50 cm)
Museum Ludwig, Cologne, Germany

vulgar, fat, or proud. Then too she captures the authority of Miss Lily Walton*** her housekeeper in the rue Cortot, whose eyes are as piercing as those of the cat Raminou; or the inspired air of Maurice Utrillo at his easel.*

Jean Vertex said: «The sensuality of this impetuous and implacable woman is expressed to the detriment of sensitivity. She detests women and takes her revenge for any charm they may have by damning them with her brush, producing a likeness which is rendered more faithful by the fact that not a single detail is neglected in idealizing them as little as possible.»

It is interesting to examine the subjects she chose for her portraits – her family, her associates, her friends and her two dogs, *Arbi and the Misse.*** While Degas and Toulouse-Lautrec painted dancers, circus people and music hall comedians, prostitutes and washerwomen, Suzanne Valadon seems to be gradually attempting to escape from her social background, turning her back on the distant period when she was the «famous» Maria, growing up as best she could in a world of poverty.

As a model who had become a painter, she was proud of having risen in the social scale, and she emphasized her new status by her portraits of respectable women: *Madame Lévy,* a businesswoman; *Madame Kars,* a painter's wife; *Madame Zamaron,* the wife of a police inspector and well-known collector; *Madame Coquiot,**** a critic's wife; and the *Rivière Ladies* covered in necklaces and bracelets. Her models have the opulence she had missed when she was young but would enjoy during the 1920s thanks to the money brought in by Utrillo. In spite of his chaotic existence as an alcoholic, Maurice was painting masterpieces which were recognized and sought after by dealers and collectors.

In 1921 the painting *The Utter Family* marks a further stage in her art. The three figures, Suzanne's mother-in-law and sister-in-law, are still shown in rigid postures like the donors in a primitve picture, but the setting, the flowers and the furniture are no longer painted without depth as they would have been ten years before. Their volume gives them an existence of their own.

STILL LIFES AND LANDSCAPES

Utter brought Suzanne his youth but also his technical knowledge of painting. She ground her pigments herself and was only too glad to have his advice. She remembered Lautrec's palette and knew how important it was to prepare the canvas correctly. According to Tabarant, Suzanne Valadon used only five colors when she first began to paint: two chrome yellows, a vermilion, a deep madder lake and zinc white. To these she added an ivory black or the bitumen which was fashionable at the time. After 1909 she extended her palette, and Geneviève Barrez, the author of a thesis on Suzanne Valadon, lists the fourteen colors the artist used toward the end of her life: the pigments mentioned above, and also yellow ocher, raw sienna, light crimson lake, Venetian red or reddish brown, cobalt blue, deep ultramarine, deep English green and emerald green. She used neither white nor pure black, and no mineral spirit but unbleached linseed oil. Black was replaced by ultramarine blue mixed with sienna, vermilion and English green, or ultramarine combined with reddish brown. Suzanne wanted her palette to be simple so that she would not have to think about it.

Everything she painted was infused with life, just as she herself was full of passion and energy and a love of truth that she expressed brutally and savagely on her canvas. «*Nature* has a complete hold over me,» she said. «Trees, sky, water and people move me deeply, passionately. It is shapes and colors and movements that have made me paint, in an attempt to render with love and fervor that which I care about so much. In what I have painted there is not a stroke or a line that is not based on *nature. Nature* is the yardstick by which I measure the truth in *building up* canvases that are conceived by me, but always motivated by the feeling of life itself.»

Suzanne Valadon meant by nature the universality and mystery of all living things.

---

* See p. 64.   ** See p. 87.   *** See p. 63.

Crouching Nude Holding the Grandmother by Her Dress, 1909
Drawing, 13" × 16 1/2" (33 × 42 cm). Private collection

She was always seeking a reason why, and was never at peace except when she fulfilled herself in her painting, at the same time satisfying her need for knowledge of herself and her curiosity about everything around her.

Suzanne Valadon's first still life, *Apples and Pear,* * painted in 1900, recalls the style of Cézanne. But the still lifes with a teapot** (1911), with a pink drapery*** (1920), or a violin (1923), as well as the many bunches of flowers (the first dated 1903), reveal a new voluptuousness and richness of texture, and colors splendid as enamels.****

Suzanne can express her sensuality in a single rose, a few bright flowers or a handful of ripe fruit. There is nothing fragile about her compositions, they are sometimes almost stifling in their density. The vases containing the flowers are solid, even the petals are heavy, and the stems grow thicker as the years go by. Suzanne loves the round full shapes of jugs and teapots. Heavy crimson draperies set off pink carnations, or a violin lying beside a case with a royal blue lining.***** Her art is anything but meticulous, and yet the heads of the dahlias, anemones

* See p. 41. ** See p. 68. *** See p. 20. **** See pp. 18, 19, 49, 78, 81, 89. *****See p. 69.

Nude Getting into the Bath beside the Seated Grandmother, 1908
Black crayon, 11 3/8" × 15 3/8" (20 × 39 cm). Private collection

and poppies are painted with the same attention as a portrait, as if each flower were personalized. And that is one of her major qualities as a painter. She never repeats herself but starts afresh every time she tackles a subject. All her senses are alert when she gazes intensely at the object she has chosen to paint. She extracts the juice, the very essence of the apple, the tree or the plant, in the same way as she captures the spirit of the animals or people who pose for her.

The first landscapes painted by Suzanne Valadon have none of the pale light of which the Impressionists are so fond, but form a rigid block like a backdrop against which appear Adam and Eve* or a group of naiads. They might be described as a brightly colored Puvis repainted by Gauguin. Very different is the style in *Joy of Living*** of 1911, where mannered nudes with emphatic gestures disport themselves in front of a young athlete (Utter) against a naturalistic background. The tree is vigorous and the ocher-colored earth blends with the bodies. The landscape fills the space and the figures play only a minor role. In *Tree at Montmagny,**** they have vanished altogether.

The *Casting of the Net***** of 1914 is a huge canvas measuring 2 meters square. A classical composition with an academic theme, it not only has a geometrical construction (position of the bodies and the nets), but also contains a realistic portrait (Utter), a study of movement recalling Matisse's *Dance,* and a setting where the pink mountain and blue lake inspired by a visit to Corsica are reminiscent of the colors used by Cézanne.

During a stay in Brittany in 1912, the artist painted the Isle of Ushant from life, in a series of stylized, compartmented pictures after the manner of Gauguin. The following year at Corte and Belgodère in Corsica, she discovered how the intense southern light could emphasize the outlines of the landscape. Her talents as a draftsman are used to pick out the hills, the cypresses, the stones in a low wall or an olive tree in the foreground.

She was fascinated by the techniques of Pont-Aven and may well have been influenced by Gauguin, Cézanne and Bazille, whose retrospective exhibitions she had seen at the Salon d'Automne. René Huyghe said that the art of Suzanne Valadon is «a product of Pont-Aven and Montmartre.» If the artists who lodged at Marie-Jeanne Gloanec's Inn revolutionized painting by their theories, Montmartre is undoubtedly the home of the Indépendants. Degas, Forain, Toulouse-Lautrec, Bottini, and Valadon never really belonged to a school, and the only thing they had in common was that they lived on the Butte.

Suzanne painted *The Sacré Cœur****** and the *Gardens of the Rue Cortot******* (1916), confining herself to what she could see from her window. The opaque white of the basilica contrasts with the shiny green of the leaves on the trees, the colors of the old tiled roofs and the soft blue of the sky. This is one of the scenes often painted by Utrillo during his white period that Suzanne admired so much. «That sky: It makes me sick . . . Yes of course, sick with joy, with jealousy, to be able to feel it so pure, so light, so fluid . . . » she said to Francis Carco and the critic Vauxcelles, proudly showing them Maurice's paintings.

She had always obliged her son to paint according to high standards inspired more by her passion as an artist than by her love as a mother. In this she showed a great deal of intelligence and common sense, never attempting to influence him but merely teaching him technique. She helped him prepare his palette and choose the colors, advising him to mix oil with the pigments instead of applying them directly from the tube. But their temperaments are reflected very differently in their art. She is thoughtful and serious-minded, while he is intuitive, morbidly sensitive, almost mystical in his approach.

Life in the rue Cortot was becoming increasingly difficult as everyone was worried about Utrillo's condition. He spent some time in the mental ward of the Sainte-Anne Hospital, and in order to obtain permission for him to leave, on August 10, 1920, his mother and stepfather had to promise the prefect of the police to keep him under constant supervision. Utter made Maurice sign a note stating: «As a result of this undertaking, I cannot let you come and

---

* See p. 36. ** See pp. 38-39. *** See p. 52. **** See pp. 42-43. ***** See p. 53.
****** See p. 56.

THE BLUE ROOM, 1923. Oil on canvas, 35 7/16″ × 45 5/8″ (90 × 116 cm)
Musée National d'Art Moderne. Centre National d'Art et de Culture Georges Pompidou, Paris

Flower in a Glass, 1932. Oil on canvas, 13″ × 9 7/16″ (33 × 24 cm)
Private collection

WOMAN WITH WHITE STOCKINGS, 1924. Oil on canvas, 28 3/4″ × 23 5/8″ (73 × 60 cm)
Musée de Nancy, France

Study for the Sleeping Black Woman, 1919
Oil on canvas, 20 7/8″ × 31 1/2″ (53 × 80 cm). Private collection

FLOWERS IN A VASE, 1927. Oil on canvas, 21 5/8″ × 18″ (55 × 46 cm). Private collection

◁
Two Nudes
or
The Bath, 1923
Oil on canvas
63 3/4″ × 51 1/8″
(162 × 130 cm)
Private collection

Nude Black
Woman, 1919
Oil on canvas
62 7/8″ × 38 1/8″
(160 × 97 cm)
Musée de Menton
France

THE CHURCH AT SAINT-BERNARD, 1929. Oil on canvas, 39 3/8″ × 31 7/8″ (100 × 81 cm)
Musée National d'Art Moderne. Centre National d'Art et de Culture Georges Pompidou, Paris

go as you please, as you are allowed out only accompanied, otherwise you will leave here for the lunatic asylum. These are the plain facts.»

While Utrillo's mental state continued to deteriorate, Suzanne herself was becoming successful. In 1920 she was made a member of the Salon d'Automne where she had been exhibiting since 1909. Her works appeared at national and international exhibitions and she was called «Valadon,» like a man, to distinguish her from conventional women painters. Her exhibitions at the Berthe Weill and John Levy galleries in 1921 received favorable notices, and the following year Bernheim-Jeune gave her a contract. The great day was celebrated by a sumptuous banquet organized by Tabarant at the Maison Rose, rue de l'Abreuvoir. The guests were her friends Francis Carco, André Warnod, the poet and publisher François Bernouard, the critic Georges Coquiot, and the painters Derain, Braque, and Pascin and his wife, Hermine David.

The money began to flow in, and Suzanne became outrageously extravagant, accumulating fur coats and hats she never wore, ordering meals for fifteen when there were only three guests, and offering enormous tips to taxi drivers and even engine drivers when she took the train to Genet in Brittany, or Ségalas in the Pyrenees, where she painted a number of luxuriant green landscapes.

Gracious living began in earnest in 1923 – it would last for ten years – when the trio went to live at Saint-Bernard, near Villefranche-sur-Saône, in a dilapidated thirteenth century castle. Only one square tower beside the ruins was still habitable.

The new lords of the manor caused a sensation in the little Beaujolais town. They arrived from Paris in an impressive Panhard driven by a liveried chauffeur. In spite of the idyllic setting, their life soon became as impossible as ever, and it was not long before the Utter-Valadon-Utrillo family was ostracized by all the neighbors. Maurice made scenes when he was forbidden alcohol. Utter grew exasperated and insulted Suzanne, while she took refuge with her dogs in the countryside, where she began to paint, entranced by the wide horizons of the region.

The artist captures the atmosphere of the banks of the Saône not by effects of light but by stark and massive volumes. In winter, once the mist has lifted, a golden light shines through the tracery of the branches of the bare trees onto the walls of the houses of Saint-Bernard. The castle and church resemble the *Jas de Bouffan* by Cézanne.*

This rural interlude in Suzanne Valadon's life was marked by the visits of Edouard Herriot, then a young deputy and mayor of Lyons, who came to the feudal dwelling as a neighbor. It was he who, in 1928, at the instigation of Francis Carco, presented Maurice Utrillo with the insignia of the Legion of Honor. Utrillo received the award ceremoniously in the castle courtyard. Edouard Herriot wrote the preface for the catalogue of Suzanne Valadon's major retrospective exhibition at the Gallery Georges Petit in 1932. Recalling the artist's magnificent and unassuming work, he describes one of her landscapes:

> «Against a sky still wet with fluid ink, the rolling hills stretch away behind a curtain of pale trees where yellow merges softly into green. The courtyard of the dwelling where the three painters work – a trinity inspired by the same cult of art – is surrounded by old, crumbling walls to which Utrillo has given a look of sadness . . . »

Suzanne Valadon had lived so long in the rue Cortot that it was not without regret she left the studio in 1926 for a small house in the avenue Junot. After having enjoyed affluence, she was once more faced with poverty. It seemed to be her destiny to be alternately poor and rich.

Her pictures were becoming increasingly difficult to sell during the Depression, and she began to paint less. The enthusiastic, dynamic Maria-Anne Camax Zoegger, president of the Salon des Femmes Artistes Modernes, finally succeeded – no easy task in view of Valadon's misogyny – in persuading her to exhibit with her fellow women artists.

Suzanne seldom went back to Saint-Bernard, where Utter was leading a depressing existence without money or friends. Having given up all hope of «putting his house in order,» he

---

* See p. 84.

ANDRÉ UTTER AND HIS DOGS, 1932. Oil on canvas, 64 1/8″ × 51 5/8″ (163 × 131 cm)
Private Collection

ARBI AND THE MISSE, 1927. Oil on wood, 13″ × 16 7/8″ (33 × 43 cm)
Private collection

stopped seeing the woman he still loved but whose formidable character he found impossible to live with. And yet she continued to wait for him in Montmartre, always leaving her door open in case he came back. But the family atmosphere had hopelessly deteriorated. Utter had met a woman named Madeleine, of whom he wrote as follows to Suzanne: «She is far too precious as a source of consolation for me to be able to contemplate no longer seeing her . . . » Another chapter had come to an end.

In 1935 Utrillo married Lucie Valore, the widow of a famous collector. This took an enormous weight off his mother's shoulders but at the same time left her feeling sad and lonely. Her neighbor the painter Naly used to go and sit with her: «This tiny woman was a bundle of nerves, and she never seemed to sleep. She would keep me awake all night talking about painting with indefatigable enthusiasm. For example she would pick up an album of Venetian art and analyze with amazing penetration and lucidity the technique of Titian and Tintoretto. She taught me everything I know.»

An old Montmartre companion, Gazi, who called her his «little mother,» took care of her and encouraged her to seek consolation in religion. She still painted nudes in memory of Puvis de Chavannes, as well as bunches of roses – one of them in a pot bearing the words «Vive la jeunesse» (long live youth).

Francis Carco went to see her shortly before she died.

«She had taken refuge in the downstairs room in the house in the avenue Junot, where she had installed a divan among the stretchers and frames that made the room look like a dusty and bizarre property room. My first impression was so vivid I was unable to dissimulate it; it was almost a year since I had seen Valadon and I had some difficulty in recognizing her. One felt that she was at the end of her strength. Her worn-out shoes, her grubby dressing gown, the strands of white hair falling over her forehead, and the deterioration in her shiny, wrinkled face made her look like an old woman whose body appeared to have shrunk . . .

«Why should I struggle? For the sake of whom? As long as I had Maurice to look after, my life had some meaning . . .

«My work? My work is finished, and the only satisfaction it gives me is never to have betrayed or surrendered anything in which I believed. You will see that is true one day, perhaps, if anyone ever takes the trouble to do me justice.»

On April 7, 1938, she died of a stroke at the age of seventy-three. Her coffin was followed to the Church of Saint-Pierre in Montmartre by her friends and all those who had championed her art, among them Edouard Herriot, Georges Huysman, then director of the Beaux-Arts, André Salmon, André Warnod, Robert Rey and Francis Carco.

Why has Suzanne Valadon's work still not achieved the success it deserves?

Her painting was probably overshadowed by Utrillo's, but other reasons seem more convincing: her total independence of both official and experimental art.

She was very young at the time when Gauguin, Emile Bernard and their friends were reacting against Impressionism at Pont-Aven, and when Degas and Toulouse-Lautrec were revolutionizing traditional realism. And when the Fauve and Cubist leaders attracted painters and poets by their avant-garde spirit, Suzanne Valadon never took part in any of these movements. Alone she accomplished a body of work that remained outside all the currents of the time and that has an audacity still appreciated today. Unwittingly, perhaps, she was even a precursor of Fauvism and Expressionism.

Bernard Dorival explains her originality: «It is probably the ease with which she was able to reconcile the two opposing aims she sought for all her life: that of beauty through the setting and character through ugliness . . . If she succeeded in harmonizing these opposites, it is for a reason that is very characteristic of her: because she never deliberately tried to reconcile the irreconcilable. And perhaps in this disregard for logic, in this inconsistency and indifference to contradictions, lies the only feminine trait in the art of Suzanne Valadon, that most virile – and the greatest – of all the women in painting.»

Today when the many new forms of realism are attracting attention, how much more convincing appears the work of Suzanne Valadon in which realism is expressed by a power of evocation that owes nothing to servile imitation, and is the exact opposite of the current flat, cold and impersonal imagery.

Suzanne Valadon affirms the permanence of a classical spirit that never declines into academism. In fact, her paintings differ so widely that it is difficult to generalize about her art. Each of her canvases has a life of its own and a style that will never become dated, because, as she never belonged to any group, everything she does is original. «To be truthful» was one of her ambitions, and she impresses us precisely because of her sincerity, her mastery of technique, and the consistency of her personal views.

«I have had some great teachers, and I have got the best out of them, in terms of both teaching and example. I have found myself, I made myself what I am, and I think that I have said what I had to say. So what would be the good of going on, repeating myself, becoming senile? No thank you, not me . . . » she said to Jean Vertex, as if she was passing judgment on her work and was aware of having expressed the essential.

To find herself. That had been the main preoccupation of the young Marie-Clémentine, at once her anxiety and her inspiration, and what she finally found was Suzanne Valadon, a great painter.

Palette of Suzanne Valadon. Bouquet of Roses in a Glass, 1931
12 5/8″ × 19 5/8″ (32 × 50 cm). Private collection

BIOGRAPHY

1865 On September 23, at six o'clock in the morning, Marie-Clémentine Valadon was born in the house of Madame Guimbaud, a widow, at Bessines-sur-Gartempe. She was the daughter of Madeleine Valadon, a thirty-four-year-old sewing maid, and of an unknown father, who probably resided in the town of Bessines.
She was christened on September 24. Her godfather was Matthieu Basbeix; her godmother was Marie-Céline Coulaud.

before 1870 She was taken as a baby to Paris, where her mother worked as a cleaning woman. They lived on the boulevard Rochechouart. Valadon may have attended a Catholic school.

1875-1880 Worked successively as a milliner's apprentice, a nanny, a waitress in a restaurant, and sold vegetables at the Batignolles market(?).

1880-1885 She lived on the rue Tourlaque and became familiar with the Montmartre of the artists. She fell from a trapeze.
She started working as a model, sitting for such artists as Puvis de Chavannes (*The Sacred Grove*, commissioned in 1883, exhibited at the 1884 Salon, now at the Musée des Beaux-Arts in Lyons), Renoir (*The Dance in Town* and *The Dance in the Country*, 1883, *The Braid*, 1885, and several *Bathers*), Henner, Inaïs *(Truth Emerging from the Well*, 1887), and Toulouse-Lautrec, her neighbor *(Portrait*, now at the Ny Carlsberg Clyptotek in Copenhagen, *The Drinker* or *Hangover*, 1889, at the Musée d'Albi . . .)

1883 First known works clearly dated: a *Self-Portrait*, in pastel, and a *Portrait of my Mother*. Valadon liked to say that she had started drawing when she was nine years old.
On December 26, Maurice Valadon was born to Marie-Clémentine and an unknown father. In 1891, Miquel Utrillo y Molins, a Spanish journalist and artist, will acknowledge him as his son. It is possible that Miquel Utrillo should be the child's father, but other names have also been suggested, among them a singer at the Lapin Agile, Boissy.

1883-1893 Many drawings (in lead pencil, charcoal and red chalk) where she showed an increasing mastery of her art. Her models came from everyday life: her son, her mother, herself, Miquel Utrillo. They are portraits and family scenes where one can detect Degas' influence. Valadon had met Degas (one does not know exactly the circumstances). In his letters (most of them undated, but they seem to spread over a period between 1890 and 1917), Degas expressed his affection for Valadon and his admiration for her work. He was one of the first to buy her drawings. He called her «his terrible Maria,» but she never posed for him as a model.

1893 She had an affair with Erik Satie, who also lived at 6 rue Cortot. She continued to draw. First known oil paintings: *Portrait of a Little Girl, Portrait of Erik Satie, Portrait of Bernard Lemaire, Telling the Child a Tale, Young Girl Doing Crochet Work*, all probably dating from around 1892.

1894 Encouraged perhaps by Degas, Valadon submitted works to the Salon de la Nationale. In an undated letter to Helleu, Bartholomé suggested that he should «look at the drawings signed Valadon when they come before the selection committee.»
She exhibited five drawings at the 1894 Salon de la Nationale: *The Toilet of the Grandson* (No. 1670), *Grandmother and Grandson* (No. 1671) and three studies of children (Nos. 1672, 1673, and 1674).

1895 In 1894 or 1895 she tried her hand at soft-ground etching in Degas' studio. Many drawings.

1896 On August 5, she married Paul Mousis, whom she seemed to have known since 1893. He was chief clerk at the firm Bel et Sainbénat and a man of means. They spent their time between a studio at 12 rue Cortot, in Montmartre, and a house in the country near Pierrefitte. It was in the country that Valadon painted *The Grandmother and the Little Rosalie*, one of the first oils since the series executed in 1882-1893.

1896-1909 She led a comfortable life. Valadon could at last devote herself to painting, and above all to drawing and etching. Her work was sold by Le Barc de Boutteville and by Vollard. The latter published her prints in 1897.
Young Utrillo, her son, was raised by his grandmother and very soon he showed the first symptoms of alcoholism. He was unable to continue attending the Collège Rollin, where he was a rather poor student. Paul Mousis found him a job for a few months as a supernumerary

at the Crédit Lyonnais bank. It is said that a doctor, Dr. Ettlinger, suggested that Valadon teach the young alcoholic to paint «as a relief from his nervous overstimulation.» «A painter against his will,» Utrillo kept drinking and he was forced to leave his parents' house.

1909 Valadon met one of her son's friends, the artist André Utter (whom she may have already met at Pierrefitte). Born in 1886, he was twenty-one years her junior. Valadon left Mousis, filed for divorce and went to live with Utter at the impasse Guelma. Later she returned to 12 rue Cortot when Emile Bernard vacated his studio.
Utter had a stimulating influence on Valadon whose extensive output showed an authority she had not achieved before. Apart from the drawings, she painted *Spring, Nude at the Mirror, After the Bath, Adam and Eve. Summer* was exhibited at the Salon d'Automne (No. 1677).

1910 Portraits: *Grandmother and Grandson.* She started painting large canvases which showed the influence of Puvis de Chavannes *(Joy of Living,* 1910).
She exhibited at the Salon d'Automne (Nos. 1159-1161).

1911 *Still Life with Teapot.* Large canvases *(The Judgment of Paris?).*
First solo show at the Clovis Sagot Gallery. *The Joy of Living* and *Hairdressing* were exhibited at the Salon d'Automne (Nos. 1605-1606) and six other works were at the Salon des Indépendants (Nos. 6073 to 6078), among which was *Grandmother and Grandson.* Valadon always claimed her predilection for the Salon des Indépendants and later she deplored its decline (cf. «Bulletin de la Vie Artistique,» February 15, 1921, pp. 108-110). Utrillo is «discovered» by Francis Jourdain, and later by Octave Mirbeau.

1912 *Family Portrait, Portrait of the Artist's Mother, The Future Unveiled, Games* 1912?).
She stayed with Utter and Utrillo in Brittany, on the Island of Ushant. Landscapes.
The Future Unveiled was shown at the Salon d'Automne (No. 1658), and three other works at the Salon des Indépendants (Nos. 3219-3221). Valadon was also part of a group show organized in Munich by Clovis Sagot.

1913 *Marie and Gilberte, Nude Having Her Hair Done,* still lifes. She stayed with Utter and Utrillo in Corsica. Good landscapes of Corte and Belgodère, painted with a very firm and precise line.
Salon d'Automne *(Young Girl at the Mirror,* No. 2020). Salon des Indépendants (Nos. 3013-3014, including *The Tub).*
Valadon participated with seven other artists in a group show at the Berthe Weill Gallery (March).

1914 The best one of her large canvases *The Casting of the Net,* was exhibited at the 1914 Salon des Indépendants. *The Seamstress* (Musée National d'Art Moderne in Paris). Still lifes and landscapes of the Oise region. In August, Utter married her before joining his army corps (158th of Infantry) at Belleville-sur-Saône. Utrillo was discharged and he went back to his mother, rue Cortot.

1915 *Portrait of Madame Gustave Coquiot.*
Solo show at Berthe Weill's.
Death of her mother.

1916 Beautiful series of nudes after the model Gaby. *Harlequin* which showed Cézanne's influence and which was painted at the same time as Utter's *Harlequin.* Flowers, landscapes of Montmartre and of the Oise region.

1917 *Rest* with Gaby as a model. Landscapes of Montmartre. In June, Valadon joined Utter who was wounded and who was recovering at the military hospital of Meyzieux. Landscapes of Nayron-le-Haut and Meyzieux.
Group show with Utter and Utrillo at the Bernheim-Jeune Gallery and at Berthe Weill's (March).

1918 *Self-Portrait* painted at Décimes. *Portrait of Madame Gebel.* Nudes.
At the end of the war, Utter returned to the rue Cortot. Valadon, whose output seemed to have slowed down during the war, is again stimulated to paint extensively.

1919 Many works. Portraits: *Utrillo Painting, The Tigress* (which showed the influence of a portrait that Renoir had painted of her), many beautiful still lifes, familiar landscapes, an important series of nudes after a mulatto model *(Black Venus, Reclining Slave).* These two paintings, along with two others, were shown at the Salon d'Automne (Nos. 1864-1867). Drawing exhibitions at Berthe Weill's.
Utrillo had his first major exhibition at Lepoutre's

1920 Very productive year. Many still lifes, showing a perfect mastery of the art. Portraits *(Victor Rey).* Nudes in a rich setting of curtains and draperies. Genre scenes *(Young Italian Girl with a Doll).*
She participated with several paintings in the exhibition of «The Young French Painting» (Manzy Joyant Gallery). One painting at the Salon d'Automne (No. 3139). She was elected secretary of the Salon.
First (?) paintings sold on auction (Hôtel Drouot, October 22 and December 16).

1921 Portraits: Utrillo, her niece Gilberte, *The Utter Family.* Nudes, landscapes. *The Cast-Off Doll.*

She stays in Beaujolais. Landscapes: *Castle at Jonchet, The Cowshed in Beaujolais, Orchard in Beaujolais.*
Group show with Utter and Utrillo at Berthe Weill's. One nude at the Salon des Indépendants (No. 3437).
Four major works at the Salon d'Automne: *Family Portrait* (No. 2372), *The Cast-Off Doll* (No. 2373), *Gilberte* (No. 2374), and *Portrait of Utrillo* (No. 2375).
In December, solo show at John Levy's: recent works. *The Casting of the Net, Adam and Eve,* and two portraits were shown at the International Exhibition of Modern Art in Geneva. Valadon's work is more and more appreciated by the public, as can be seen from the growing number of exhibitions and reviews (written by Robert Rey, André Warnod, Tabarant and others).

1922 Portraits: Lily Walton, Madame Zamaron, Germaine Utter, Madame Lévy. Nudes, still lifes, landscapes of Montmartre.
Stayed at Genet, in Brittany. Landscapes.
Two paintings at the Salon des Indépendants (Nos. 3582-3583), two at the Salon d'Automne (Nos. 2247).
Two Valadon and Utrillo exhibitions at Berthe Weill's (April and July).
Valadon-Utrillo-Utter exhibition at the Dalpayrat Gallery, in Limoges (May-June).
Robert Rey publishes a study which stresses Valadon's growing reputation.

1923 *The Blue Room, Self-Portrait.* Large nudes and still lifes.
Holidays with the family of the painter Georges Kars, at Ségalas, near Orthez, in the Low Pyrenees. Landscapes.
Valadon bought a castle at Saint-Bernard, in the Saône valley. Valadon, Utrillo and Utter each had their own studio. They spent their time between Saint-Bernard and Paris.
Major Valadon-Utrillo show at the Bernheim-Jeune Gallery.
Two paintings at the Salon des Indépendants (Nos. 4598-4599). One nude and *Still Life with Pineapple* at the Tuileries (Nos. 994-995). *The Blue Room* and *Still Life with Game* at the Salon d'Automne (Nos. 1955-1956). She also participated in several group exhibitions. Although she was not as successful as Utrillo, and she did not try to be, her reputation was growing. The family had a car and servants, and their life was a strange mixture of Bohemia and luxury.

1924 Large output of portraits, nudes, and still lifes. First landscapes of Saint-Bernard, which she will henceforth paint often.
Valadon may be too much in demand. She exhibited rarely. A few paintings at the Berthe Weill and Bernheim-Jeune galleries. She signed her first contract with Bernheim-Jeune. On that occasion Tabarant organized a banquet in her honor at the Maison Rose. Shows *Madame Fontaine and Her Daughter* at the Salon des Indépendants.

1925 Valadon-Utrillo-Utter exhibition at the Bernheim-Jeune Gallery. Two paintings at the Indépendants (Nos. 3343-3344).

1926 On behalf of Utrillo, Bernheim bought a house at 12 avenue Junot, where the whole family could settle.

1927 Nudes, still lifes, landscapes of Saint-Bernard. Retrospective exhibition at Berthe Weill's (January), with a foreword to the catalogue written in free verse by Berthe Weill. The show was very well received. Four paintings at the Salon des Tuileries (Nos. 2347 to 2350).

1928 Beautiful series of nudes and still lifes.
Many group exhibitions, among others in Amsterdam and New York. Two paintings at the Salon d'Automne (Nos. 2480-2481). Solo shows at the Galerie des Archers in Lyons (January) and at Berthe Weill's (April). She had become internationally known, and this success was confirmed by the publication of an illustrated article in a German journal, «Deutsche Kunst und Dekoration» (April). The following year Adolphe Basler wrote a monograph on Valadon, published by Crès.

1929 Major landscapes of Saint-Bernard.
Two shows at the Bernier Gallery: a retrospective of drawings and prints, including more or less one hundred works, with a foreword to the catalogue written by Robert Rey (January-February); recent works.

1930 Many still lifes, nudes, landscapes of Saint-Bernard.
Participates in the show «Living Art» organized at the Théâtre Pigalle.

1931 Touching *Self-Portrait with Bare Breasts, Woman Putting Shoes on a Little Girl, Woman Dressing a Little Girl* (Paris, Georges Petit, 1932). Many still lifes, landscapes at Saint-Bernard.
Participated in the exhibition of the School of Paris held in Prague. Show of recent works at the Galerie Le Portique (the catalogue has a foreword by Edouard Herriot). Major retrospective exhibition in Brussels, at the Galerie Le Centaure.

1932 *Portrait of André Utter with his Dogs.* Still lifes and landscapes of Saint-Bernard.
Valadon had her most important retrospective exhibition at the Georges Petit Gallery. Edouard Herriot wrote the foreword to the catalogue. The show was well received by the press but there were almost no sales.
Exhibition of drawings and prints at the Galerie

Le Portique. Group exhibition Utrillo-Valadon-Utter at the Moos Gallery, in Geneva, where Valadon showed around one hundred paintings. Daragnès published a luxurious book of the complete engraved works by Valadon. The foreword and the catalogue were by Claude Roger-Marx. The book did not sell well.

1933 Valadon seemed to paint less. Those who knew her in those days recount her tiredness, her fits of nihilism relieved by sudden outbursts of high spirits. She mostly painted flowers and she did not go to Saint-Bernard anymore.
Laden with glory, Utrillo became naively mystical. On June 8, he was christened and he took to the most fervent religion.
Although she disliked «women's art,» Valadon accepted the invitation of Marie-Anne Camax Zoegger to participate in the Salon des Femmes Artistes Modernes, where she was to exhibit until she died.

1934 She saw Utter irregularly. Around the same time, she developed a loving friendship with a painter called Gazi, who called her his «little mother.» He awakened in her a religious sensitivity that she had not felt since childhood.

1935 Sick with diabetes and uremia, Valadon was treated at the American Hospital in Neuilly, near Paris. It is said that she then advised Lucie Valore to marry Utrillo. Lucie Valore was the widow of Robert Pauwels, a Belgian banker and a collector of Utrillo's paintings. Utrillo left, but not without painful upheavals.

1936 Still lifes with flowers that bear moving dedications.

1937 The State bought several paintings for the Musée du Luxembourg (which already owned *The Blue Room* and a still life now in the collection of the Musée des Beaux-Arts in Grenoble), among which are *The Casting of the Net, Adam and Eve, Grandmother and Grandson,* as well as several drawings. The French national museums have a magnificent collection of works by Valadon, which is now on view at the National Museum of Modern Art in Paris.

1938 Valadon died suddenly of a stroke, at the Piccini Hospital, on April 7, at eleven o'clock in the morning. There was a funeral service at the church of Saint-Pierre in Montmartre. Utter was the chief mourner.

From the catalogue written by Pierre Georgel for the Valadon exhibition held in 1967 at the Musée National d'Art Moderne, in Paris.

BIBLIOGRAPHY

WORKS QUOTED IN THE TEXT

BARREZ, Geneviève: *Suzanne Valadon.* Doctoral Dissertation, unpublished, Ecole du Louvre, Paris.
BAZIN, Germain: *Histoire de l'Art contemporain: la Peinture.* Paris, 1935.
CARCO, Francis: *Le Nu dans la peinture moderne.* Editions Crès, Paris, 1924.
L'Ami des peintres. Gallimard, Paris, 1953.
DORIVAL, Bernard: *Les Etapes de la peinture française contemporaine. De l'Impressionnisme au Fauvisme.* Gallimard, Paris, 1943.
GAUZI, François: *Toulouse-Lautrec et son temps.* David Perret, Paris, 1954 (Collection «La Bibliothèque des Arts»).
MERMILLON, Marius: *Le Trio Saint-Bernard.* Lettres Françaises, 3 Juillet 1948.
PROU, Suzanne: *Suzanne Valadon.* Catalogue Franska Instituted, Stockholm, 1978.
ROGER-MARX, Claude: *Les Dessins de Suzanne Valadon.* Eighteen original prints by Suzanne Valadon, executed between 1895 and 1910, with a preface and a catalogue. Daragnès, Paris, 1932.
TABARANT, André: *Suzanne Valadon et ses souvenirs de modèle.* Bulletin de la Vie artistique, Paris, December 15, 1921. 626-629.
VALADON, Suzanne and BAZIN, Germain: *Suzanne Valadon par elle-même.* Prométhée, Paris, March 1939.
VERTEX, Jean: *Le Village inspiré.* Jean Vertex, 1950.
WARNOD, André: *L'Avenir.* December 19, 1921.
Ceux de la Butte. Julliard, Paris, 1947.
MUSÉE NATIONAL D'ART MODERNE: Catalogue by Pierre Georgel. Preface by Bernard Dorival. Notes by Robert Le Masle. Paris, 1967.

BOOKS

APOLLINAIRE, Guillaume: *Chronique d'art 1902-1918.* Gallimard, Paris, 1960.

BANLIN-LACROIX, Catherine: *Miquel Utrillo y Molins,* critique d'art. Paris University, IV. Doctoral dissertation, October 1971.

BASLER, Adolphe: *Suzanne Valadon.* Crès, Paris, 1929. (Collection «Les Artistes nouveaux»).

BEACHBOARD, Robert: *La Trinité maudite, Utter, Valadon, Utrillo.* Amiot-Dumont, Paris, 1952.

BONNAT, Yves: *Valadon.* Club d'art Bordas, Paris, 1968.

COQUIOT, Gustave: *Cubistes, Futuristes, Passéistes.* Librairie Ollendorf, Paris, 1914.
Les Indépendants, Paris, 1921.

COURTHION, Pierre: *Montmartre.* Skira, Geneva, 1956. (Collection «Le Goût de notre temps»).

CRESPELLE, Jean-Paul: *La Vie quotidienne à Montmartre.* Hachette, Paris, 1978.
Utrillo. Presses de la Cité, Paris, 1970.
Montmartre vivant. Hachette, Paris, 1964.

DAUBERVILLE, Henry: *La Bataille de l'Impressionnisme.* Bernheim-Jeune, Paris, 1967.

DORGELÈS, Roland: *Bouquet de Bohème.* Albin Michel, Paris, 1947.

DORIVAL, Bernard: *The School of Paris in the Musée d'Art Moderne.* Harry N. Abrams, New York, 1962.
Twentieth-Century Painters. Universe Books, New York, 1958.

FELS, Florent: *Maurice Utrillo.* Librairie de France, Paris, 1930.
Le Roman de l'art vivant. Fayard, Paris, 1959.

HUISMAN, P. and DORTU, C.: *Lautrec par Lautrec.* Bibliothèque des Arts, Paris, 1964.

HUYGHE, René: *Les Puissances de l'image.* Flammarion, Paris, 1965.

JACOMETTI, Nesto: *Suzanne Valadon.* Pierre Cailler, Geneva, 1947.

MAC ORLAN, Pierre: *Montmartre. Souvenirs.* Chabassol, Brussels, 1946.

MATHEY, François: *Six femmes peintres: Berthe Morisot, Eva Gonzalès, Séraphine Louis, Suzanne Valadon, Marie Laurencin.* Editions du Chêne, Paris, 1951.

MERMILLON, Marius: *Suzanne Valadon, 1867-1938.* Braun, Paris, 1950. («Collection des maîtres»). Text in French, English and German.

MONNERET, Sophie: *L'Impressionnisme et son époque* (4 volumes). Denoël-Filippachi, Paris, 1980.

MUNSTERBERG, Hugo: *A History of Women Artists.* Clarkson N. Potter, Inc., New York, 1975.

NATANSON, Thadée: *Un Toulouse-Lautrec.* Pierre Cailler, Geneva, 1961.

PETERSEN, Karen and WILSON, J.: *Women Artists.* Harper & Row, New York, 1976.

PÉTRIDÈS, Paul: *Catalogue raisonné de l'œuvre de Suzanne Valadon* et *Avant propos.* Compagnie français des Arts graphiques, Paris, 1971.

RAYNAL, Maurice: *Modern French Painters.* Brentano, New York.

REY, Robert: *Suzanne Valadon.* Editions de la «Nouvelle Revue Française,» Paris, 1922. (Collection «Les Peintres français nouveaux»).

SALMON, André: *L'An de la Butte,* Paris, 1945.

STORM, John: *The Valadon Drama.* E.P. Dutton & Co., New York, 1959.

TABARANT, André: *Utrillo.* Bernheim-Jeune, Paris, 1926.

Warnod, André: *Les Berceaux de la jeune peinture: Montmartre - Montparnasse.* Albin-Michel, Paris, 1925.
Les Peintres de Montmartre. Paris, 1928.
Fils de Montmartre. Fayard, Paris, 1955.
Drôle d'époque. Souvenirs. Fayard, Paris, 1960.

WEILL, Berthe: *Pan dans l'œil* (1900-1930). Librairie Lipschutz, Paris, 1933.

YAKI, Paul: *Le Montmartre de nos vingt ans.* Tallandier, Paris, 1933.

CATALOGUES

MUSÉE NATIONAL D'ART MODERNE: Jean Cassou. Paris, 1948.

HAUS DES KUNST: Paul Pétridès. Munich, 1960.

MUSÉE DE L'AIN: *Utrillo, Valadon, Utter, Période de Saint-Bernard.* Françoise Baudson. Brou, 1965.

METROPOLITAN MUSEUM OF ART: *Impressionism, a Centenary Exhibition.* New York, 1974-75. Chapter Renoir: Michel Hoog.

LOS ANGELES COUNTY MUSEUM OF ART: *Women Painters: 1550-1950.* Ann Sutherland Harris and Linda Nochlin. Los Angeles, 1976.

MAISONS DES ARTS ET DES LOISIRS: Sochaux. Foreword by Pierre Georgel, 1976.

GRAND-PALAIS: *Puvis de Chavannes.* Notes by Louise d'Argencourt. Paris, 1976.

MUSÉE TOULOUSE-LAUTREC: *Maurice Utrillo, Suzanne Valadon.* Michel Castel, Jean De Voisins, Jean-Alain Meric. Albi, 1979.

GALERIE BERTHE WEILL: Paris, 1927.

GALERIE DES ARCHERS: Adolphe Basler and Marius Mermillon, Lyons, 1928.

GALERIE BERNIER: *Drawings and Etchings.* Robert Rey, Paris, 1928.

GALERIE LE PORTIQUE: Edouard Herriot, Paris, 1931.

GALERIE GEORGES PETIT: Edouard Herriot, 1932.

GALERIE PÉTRIDÈS: Jean Bouret, Paris, 1947.

ARTICLES

BACHELIER, Odette: *Le vieux Montmartre.* Vol. 41. Paris, December 1979.
BAROTTE, René: *Suzanne Valadon.* L'Art et les artistes. Paris, January 1937.
Beaux-Arts: Special issue on Suzanne Valadon. April 15, 1938.
BESSON, Georges: *Hommage à Suzanne Valadon.* Lettres françaises, June 3, 1948.
COLOMBIER, Pierre du: *Suzanne Valadon.* Amour de l'art, No. 9, September 1926.
La Gloire de Suzanne Valadon. Beaux-Arts, February 23, 1942.
COUGHLAN, Robert: *Dark Wine of Genius.* Life, No. 28, January 16, 1950.
FLORISOONE, Michel: *Suzanne Valadon.* Amour de l'art, Vol. 20, No. 4, May 1938.
GUENNE, Jacques: *Suzanne Valadon.* Art vivant, No. 159, April 1932.
LECLERE, Gaston: *12 rue Cortot.* Revue Montmartre, Paris, 1976.
Maria of Montmartre. Time, No. 67, May 28, 1956.

We wish to thank the owners of the pictures, as well as those collectors who did not want to have their names mentioned. Our special thanks to the Galerie Pétridès in Paris for their valuable and kind assistance.

MUSEUMS

FRANCE

Musée de Besançon.
Musée Municipal de Limoges.
Musée de Lyon.
Musée de Menton.
Musée de Nancy.
Musée d'Art Moderne de la Ville de Paris.
Musée National d'Art Moderne, CNAC Georges Pompidou, Paris.
Musées Nationaux, France.

GERMANY

Museum Ludwig, Cologne.

SWITZERLAND

Petit Palais, Geneva.

USA

The Detroit Institute of Arts.
Fogg Art Museum, Cambridge, Mass.
The Metropolitan Museum of Art, New York.
Museum of Art, Carnegie Institute, Pittsburgh, Penn.

PRIVATE COLLECTIONS

Jean-Claude Bellier, Paris – Oscar Ghez, Geneva – F. Peter Model, New York – Dina Vierny, Paris.